In My Father's House

House

The Family of God or Religious Mafia?

Amanda Wells

DESTINY IMAGE EUROPE
Via Maiella, 1
66020 San Giovanni Teatino (Ch) - Italy

E-mail: info@eurodestinyimage.com

ISBN: 88-900588-6-2

First printing: 2003

This book and all other Destiny Image Europe books are available at Christian bookstores and distributors worldwide.

Direct all correspondence and order products to:

DESTINY IMAGE EUROPE
Corso V. Emanuele II, 10
65121 Pescara - Italy
Tel. +39 085 4220170 – Fax: +39 085 4220168
E-mail: ordini@eurodestinyimage.com

Or reach us on The Internet:

www.eurodestinyimage.com

CONTENTS

Acknowledgments

There are so many involved when you write a book. However, the greatest acknowledgment and thanks must go to the Lord Jesus Christ. Without His love and encouragement, this day would have never come.

To my husband Roger, and four children for their love, support, encouragement and input. Love you!

To my best friend Donna, for forty years you have encouraged and drawn the best out of me.

To our friends Greg and Penny, your encouragement has kept me going.

Pastor Dwight and Geraldine Hicks, you believed in me as a woman in ministry, thank you.

To Lillian Calabria, who started to proof read this book long before it was finished; a wonderful friend who went home early to be with the Lord.

To Dr. Jonathan David, thank you for your impartation and friendship over the past years without which I would never have put pen to paper.

To Philip and Else DuPont, you are wonderful friends and awesome colleagues. Thanks to all your church for releasing you… what a crew!

To Sam and Dalene, the tears, laughter, talks, truer friends I am not sure I will meet.

Jeanette and Ian, you walked the road before us, then took our hand and helped us back, for all the laughs and haven't there been many?

To Peter and Danae, your friendship is a treasure and one we hold dear. I have gleaned so much from your lives.

To all my ministerial colleagues, who have supported Roger and I over the years.

Preface

It was a hot Australian summer and as I lay on my living room floor desperately crying out to God, the floor became wet with my tears. My cry was that He would send me a father and revelation to go with it.

I had been in a wonderful church with an awesome pastor for fifteen years, one where the Word of Faith was preached and the Spirit was free to move. Then what was missing? What was this cry coming from my very being, from the heart of a son?

That prayer started me on a journey, not just a spiritual one but a physical one! We, as a family, moved continents and I was about to comprehend in days to come that this journey was really about discovering the Apostolic and also finding the Spiritual fathers in the Body of Christ.

In the last few years as I began this adventure, I have seen in the Body, the legacy of pain and hurt that has been left, the knowledge of this subject having not been tackled comprehensively, yet as we walk into all the revelation there for us. After seeing so many in the Body of Christ hurt because of this issue, I felt it is time to write what the Lord had given me.

When Paul cried to the Corinthian church, "Where are the fathers?" his heart's desire was for the mature men in the Body to rise up and manifest the heart of the heavenly Father. Spiritual fathers are in no way to replace our heavenly Father or the intimate relationship we are to have with Him. Spiritual fathering is a process whereby the pattern, structure and design of the heavenly family are to be reproduced here on earth, thereby reforming the earth to its original creation and design.

This is not a book for the lighthearted. I wanted truth and honesty, as it is time that much of what we have done to our fathers and to so many sons, be exposed! I have tried to cover as much as I could but had to stop as there continues so much revelation about this whole subject. This book is not written as an easy to read paper back, but it has been written as a manual, particularly for pastors and leaders in mind.

Spiritual fathering must not become just another "in" word or "new move" blessing. If fathering does not achieve or affect anything, then perhaps we need to re-look at the structure that we ourselves have built, and dismantle all the man made operations.

It must be a concept that brings men and women into realignment, repositioning them and teaching them to come into a new position in God, that has been built by those ahead.

As Isaiah 61 says, *"They shall rebuild the old ruins and repair the ruined cities"*. The desolation of many generations and the sons of foreigners will feed their flocks. As we build this concept into our churches, let us not allow it to become just a sloppy love affair with a new move that will affect nothing and hurt many.

Let the fathers also take a realistic and truthful look at themselves. We have had "nice" but now we need truth. If they are incapable of all that the process entails, let them be mature enough to admit that they have not walked into the manhood yet but have needed to be able to carry this new move.

Too many men of God today are deceived into building a pedestal whereby, they have to keep other men from either dethroning them or climbing on board with them. This is not about pride and arrogance. Let it never become about numbers, who has more. Let this apostolic move be about lives and the shaping of men and women into their God given call and destinies, who leave an inheritance and legacy for our sons and daughters to walk in.

If you are a spiritual father today and have found yourself in covenant with a son, I thank you for the pain, the tears, the hurt and the laughter. Without you, a generation would lose the revelation of their inheritance. Words cannot express how much appreciation is felt from this son, for it was you who made it possible for me "to come home."

This book is hard at times but there are no apologies. Let us not say "I connect," but in truth only connect as long as all is well and we benefit.

If you are faint hearted, then this book is not for you. If you are a Pharisee building a religious institution, then please put the book away immediately, you will find much to criticize in its contents.

If on the other hand you desperately want more from your church, more from your meetings, more than building a kingdom where a man can rule, but instead, where a family is birthed, where we relate and grow... read on.

This is the day we must ask ourselves, "What are we building? Are we building a family in the pattern of the eternal family in Heaven, or are we building a Religious Mafia?"

If your heart is to find a family and connect, then read on and be blessed!

ground, natural and found much to criticize. In its confu...

... the sky. and you desperately want more from your
... more than your c... ... rather than becoming a disgusted
a wise man who has missed ... whose ...mind is bitter... When

Introduction
What Is a Son?

Today we are hearing many references made to the "apostolic move" in the church. As this apostolic dimension is revealed, then the five-fold ministry and leaders of today must have an understanding of it so they can impart into the leaders, the sons of tomorrow.

As the fullness of the apostolic dimension is released to the church, then a greater understanding of apostolic fathering must also be realized. It is impossible to have one without the other, for apostles are fathers.

God's final words in the Old Testament were possibly the most significant for us, the Church today.

> *I will turn the hearts of the fathers to the sons and the hearts of the sons to the fathers before the coming of the great and dreadful day of the Lord* (Malachi 4:5,6).

Then the Son of God came to the earth through a virgin womb. Before Jesus splits the virgin skies, the greatest spiritual awakening in the history of mankind will take place. The hearts of the fathers will be turned to the sons in the natural and in the Church.

Today's leaders must understand the dynamics of fathering so as to build the pattern of Heaven here on Earth. Ephesians 3:15 says, *"We are named after the family of Heaven and Earth."* If we are named, this means we have the same character, pattern, nature and DNA as the family of Heaven. We must have a revelation of Heaven's family so as to copy the pattern here on earth.

The Dynamic of Heaven–Sons

The word "son" is used in the following pages. Why? Are there no spiritual daughters?

Of course! Can't daughters have spiritual fathers? Of course they can, and a spiritual father can have a daughter. But here we are talking about a woman's position, her position in Him that is. Therefore we must realize that, because of her position in Him, this now causes God not to have daughters. He has sons!

> *For as many as are led by the Spirit of God, these are the sons of God* (Romans 8:14).

If God has sons and daughters, then He would be hierarchical and discriminative because sons receive the inheritance and the family name. Therefore as we can see, positionally speaking, God doesn't have a daughter, He has a son, and although we have endeavored to continue to write along this line, we are not meaning to be discriminatory toward women but to call them as God sees them, sons.

> *...And they stood before Moses... and before the elders... saying... "Our father died in the wilderness... and he had no sons"* (to plead for the inheritance) (Numbers 27:2-3).

In this scripture we see the daughters of Zelophchad, whose heritage we find in verse 1, were the sons of a son, going back to Joseph.

Zelophehad's name in Hebrew comes from the root word *echad*, which means "united", "unity", "unify" and *"Connected"*.

This man was connected to his heritage and to the past generations. Because of the revelation of connection that his parents had when he was named, this now sanctioned his daughters to enter into a dimension that changed the laws that had already been instituted by God. Zelophehad died without having sons. It was a son to whom he must legally leave the inheritance. These daughters confronted Moses, Eleazar the priest, and the princes of the congregation by the door of the tabernacle to plead their case. If a man dies because of his own sin and not in rebellion, why then shouldn't his daughters be treated as a son would?

The Lord told Moses that from that time on, it was to be made a statute of judgement for the children of Israel forever, that the daughters receive the inheritance, legacy and heritage the same as if a man had a first born son to leave it to.

> *...according to the commandment of the Lord, he gave them an inheritance among their father's brothers* (Joshua 17:4).

Zelophehad became a prominent man in Scripture. For he had five daughters who petitioned Moses and the priest, that when it came to the inheritance and a woman's heritage then she was to be treated the same as a son.

If their father Zelophehad had not been "connected" to the past generation, then his daughters would never have had the revelation of the legal right to request the statute of judgements and laws to be changed for woman eternally. Now a woman has the legal right and decree to stand before the Lord and be spiritually positioned in the same standing as a son.

> ...the daughters of Zelophehad were married... and the inheritance remained in the tribe... (Numbers 36:11,12).

A Son Exposes Religion in Any House

When a son enters a church, the spirit that is on the son, the Spirit of Adoption, will expose the lack of family within a church. A son will expose the "sons of the religious". The spirit that is on a son upsets and exposes religion–a works mentality–within a house.

When Jesus went into his Father's house, He always upset the religious people.

> For every house is built by someone, but He who builds all things is God. And Moses indeed was faithful in all His house as a servant. ...But Christ (was faithful) as a Son over His own house, whose house we are (Hebrews 3:4-6).

Saul and David were both kings, but the difference was Saul reigned as a king, whereas David, also king, reigned as a son.

Saul reigned, and David served and then scripture goes on to say that of David's descendants, there was always one on the throne.

Sons bring forth descendants, the next generation and sons leave a legacy.

After Saul was appointed king, Samuel said to Israel that the people would now live by regulations and laws. Perhaps we as a body, will also have to live by the structure we build. If it is our kingdom, then rules and regulations will be our portion.

Let Our Cry be..., "God Make Me a True Son"

To Timothy, my true son in the faith (1 Timothy 1:2).

Paul called Timothy his "true" son in the faith. Paul clarified that there is a fine line between true sons and false sons.

Although we will look at the characteristics of true spiritual sons, we must remember that sonship is a process and a son walks through the process, he doesn't just arrive. If we expect our sons to have all these characteristics, we will put unreal expectations upon them that they can't attain to, and it will bring them frustration and condemnation.

As a son walks through this process, he will gradually progress into these characteristics. We must remember the goal of reaching his destiny is the objective every son has within his heart, and with the help of a loving father, will one day attain it.

Chapter One

The Kingdom: the Very Core of Spiritual Fathering

For generations the church's major function has been to "cultivate" a local center of operations. By growing numerically and by providing many diversified meetings, which we excused as keeping the needs of our parishioners appeased, we believed we were building the church.

Today, a message is sweeping the nations as revival breathes life into the church, and with it comes a message that Jesus preached... *KINGDOM.*

> *Then He said, "To what can we liken the kingdom of God? It is like a mustard seed which... is smaller than all the seeds on earth... It grows up and becomes greater than all the herbs, and shoots out large branches, so the birds of the air may nest under its shade"* (Mark 4:30-32).

Jesus explains the concept of the kingdom; a mustard seed, the smallest and most innocuous of seeds.

This small seed has within it the potential to burst into life and then bring about multiplication from within it. To do so, the seed must first go through the process of death and the loss of its identity. When it has endured isolation, its destiny is finally reached.

The seed is more powerful than the soil, or even the environment. It has a destiny to produce life and something that will eventually be bigger and greater than the seed itself.

When the seed and soil connect and come into agreement, then a life force that has the ability to touch generations begins.

The seed, within its smallness, has the power to connect to a source greater than itself. Its beginnings are minute but as it dies within the ground and subjects itself to the process, it is suddenly connected to a succession greater than itself. Now it is no longer a seed but a tree with a root system, branches, leaves etc. that not only brings life to itself, but is also the source of life for more than itself, as a seed alone.

The Message of Connection, the Message of Kingdom.

The kingdom of God is the same as the seed. What looks externally like a small and innocuous message, is a message that advances and invades all other systems. Religious systems and even our cultures can't withhold the kingdom, for the message of kingdom is the message of connection.

A seed has its identity in itself alone, but as the seed connects to another source, its identity is no longer in itself alone, but in something greater.

Jesus said, *"I will build my church."* The church He speaks of is not a building, it is not even a group of people meeting together with a common purpose, but it is His Body.

The church is a living, breathing organism, with each part connected, bringing life to each cell. For us to have a narrow-minded view of the church, prevents us from connecting to the to life source that has been provided for us by God Himself. It prevents us from connecting to the covenant, the divinely positioned life source that fastens us to heaven.

As we allow the process of connection to occur, we then allow the Kingdom to invade and permeate our homes, our cities and our nations. The only way we stop the Kingdom from touching us is if we disconnect from each other. The Kingdom doesn't discriminate when it connects, it touches you, it will possess you, it will bring every tribe and every tongue together and into the knowledge of Christ. It will survive through anyone who will submit to the will of the Father.

For us to cry, *"Your kingdom come and Your will be done"* and not allow the process of connection to have its full and complete work, is futile.

If we do not remain connected and submitted to the Head of Heaven, then we will not have revelation of the process of connection to our God given, divinely provided relationships.

The connections that are afforded us connect us to a higher dimension and facet of heaven than we can acquire with our insular belief system. When we disconnect from either the Head, being Jesus, or our God given connections, it is mainly through hardness of heart that has usually come through offense, or because we have difficulty with submission. We can be guilty of being offended because of the Word's sake or offended through someone else's words or actions.

Connection happens in one of two places, in the heart or in the head. When we are connected via our head it is because we have an opinion! We like that person, we like his preaching, the way he dresses, or his hair etc. Opinion is not truth, it is hearsay, and each person's opinion is different and therefore is not reality. When we are connected in our heart, we are connected by truth, and truth is Christ Himself. When we connect in the head, we have an opinion, when we connect in our heart we will have action. This is the kingdom of God in function.

Connection, the Key to the Kingdom

All of creation is connected. Nothing exists or can survive in isolation. God made His creation to be connected.

Therefore a man shall leave his father and mother and be joined to his wife, and they shall become one flesh (Genesis 2:24).

"At last!" Adam cried, "She is part of my own flesh and bone! She will be called woman, because she was taken out of man."

Connection is the basis for unity; unity cannot take place without connection. Unless we, like Adam, encompass the revelation that we are bone of bone and flesh of each other's flesh, we cannot expect to walk in the concept of unity.

Unity is not "gathering together" but it is when we draw together with a common purpose, with connection being the ground that attracts us collectively so that we become one and our shared destiny can be accomplished.

Noah was told to take two of every kind of creature; God Himself is not isolated, He is Father, Son and Holy Spirit; He is connected even within Himself.

Nature itself is connected,

Leaves are connected to a tree,

Flowers to a stem,

Fish are even connected to the water that gives life to them.

Just as there is a law of connection in place for nature, God positioned a law of connection for His creation, man. Is this surprising? If God placed a law there for His creation so that it continues to be connected to the source of existence, why wouldn't He put a law in place for His most excellent creation, man?

When we speak about the law of connection, we must remember the highest connection, which is God to man through salvation, and then man to woman in marriage.

When Adam sinned, he disconnected himself from the intimate relationship he had with God. This caused the human race to spin into chaos, and death reigned. The moment Adam and Eve ate from the wrong tree, they severed their attachment with life itself. They started the death process by dying inwardly. Death reigned and God said to Adam, *"In dying you will die,"* meaning the process of death was now initiated in his body.

Death entered the earth through disconnection. To this day the enemy knows the power of the law of connection and the power in breaking it. He will still try to get us to break it and work against it rather than work with it, as there is great power and authority in connection. Now, not only were Adam and Eve disconnected from their life source, but the generations to come were also.

The next example we see of breaking the law of a God ordained connection was in the break down of a relationship between two brothers.

...Where is Abel your brother? I do not know. Am I my brother's keeper? (Genesis 4:9).

Of course, Cain knew the answer was yes. That is why he asked such an obvious question to God; Cain knew the law of a provisional (one who provides life and sustenance) connection/relationship. Why do we call it a law? The answer is simple because to break a system that God has put in place has consequences, death. For it to have consequences upon the breaking of it must therefore make it a law. When Cain rose up and killed Abel, death occurred.

We now find a disconnected person wandering the earth with no home. Neither he, nor his descendants were to ever become part of God's ultimate plan and destiny in the redemption of man. They were never to become part of the genealogy of Christ.

Today, so many Christians are wandering from church to church with nowhere to call home, with no spiritual family, no spiritual father, and no heritage to inherit or to pass on to the next generation. They have no revelation that their wandering is the process of disconnection It allows the enemy legal territory to prohibit God's power increase and authority to flow through their lives.

God has ordained to each one of us provisional relationships, but more importantly, a father of the house, thus the reason for this manual. As we shed light on the subject, we can walk through the process with greater ease than those who went blindly before us May this book relieve some of the pain of ignorance for those sons to come.

The righteous shall flourish like palm trees, they shall grow like cedars in Lebanon. Those who are planted in the house of the Lord shall flourish in the courts of our God. They shall still bear fruit in old age... (Psalm 92:12-14).

In the Hebrew flourish is an interesting word: Parach; to breakthrough and forth as a bud when it blooms, to flourish, to blossom abundantly, and to grow.

Today, we hear so much about **breakthrough**. In essence, breakthrough is God wanting us to permanently break free from our cycles of death, defeat, and our religious, cultural and social obstacles.

These restrain us from breaking through and being free to break out into our societies, cities and nations.

> *The righteous shall flourish like the palm tree: they shall grow like a cedar in Lebanon* (Psalm 92:12).

The righteous breakthrough like the palm tree, which is erect, sturdy in its structure, with boundaries having strength and intensity. They will grow, enlarge and increase like a cedar of Lebanon. Why this tree?

The cedar of Lebanon speaks of the heart or the core of man and this tree is recognized for its amazing root firmness and system.

The next verse is the key to breakthrough and maturity.

> *Those who are planted in the house of the Lord shall flourish* in the courts of our God (Psalm 92:13).

Being planted and producing fruit means **LIFE** is being produced in your life. You are connected to a system and your root system is healthy. It is to produce fruit, not gifts or signs and wonders, but the fruit of a changed life.

Many Christians think that attending church is connecting, and being planted.

WRONG! Why?

Attending is not attaching and coming is not connecting. You cannot build a relationship on this concept.

Being planted means the plant gives of itself and is connected to its parts, to its roots, leaves etc. It doesn't just associate with its parts when it's in the mood or feels like it. When the leaves fall off in autumn, the plant doesn't throw a pity party; it stays connected to the system, no matter what.

Those that be transplanted... (Original Hebrew)

The word **transplanted** in this psalm is a carefully chosen word. To transplant means you relocate, transfer, uproot and resettle, but most interestingly, you **reposition (to take out of its previous place of settlement and put into a new one).** When we look at this psalm, the writer is saying, those who allow themselves to be repositioned and connected to another source, can and will breakthrough.

You can attend a church for fifty years and never breakthrough. It is only when you allow yourself to be repositioned and connected to a life source that you can possibly breakthrough and grow into the maturity and the destiny prepared for you.

In the house of the Lord... The Hebrew word for "House" means family; to become a son.

This is an interesting statement by the psalmist when studied. "For those who are transplanted" are those who are connected into the family, and coming as a son, will breakthrough.

A leaf, a branch or fruit does not separate itself from a tree and still expect to remain alive. Why then do we?

As we remain connected to the source of life, God has provided for us in a God given family, we then live on the benefits that the relationship provides for us, legally.

Connecting = Adding!

...The Lord added to the church daily... (Acts 2:47).

People in the world join something; this is a worldly concept! God adds to us and adding is the language of increase and partnership.

When something is added, it means it enhances what we already have, but if a person joins us, they don't necessarily add anything eternal to us. People who join us can leave at any time. People who connect to us, know they are subject to a law, they cannot leave. Divine placement is not friendship where our surface and emotional desires are met. Divinely placed connections in our lives are in covenant with us, they can't leave unless they are sent.

A person who has been divinely placed in our life, and is connected, wants to be a part of the answer. They have paid the price of sacrifice and now have the privilege of shaping it.

> *From that time, many of His disciples went back and walked with Him no more. Then Jesus said to the twelve, "Do you also want to go away?" Then Simon Peter answered Him, "Lord, to whom shall we go? You have the words of eternal life"* (John 6:68).

Peter knew the power of connection. When everyone else left and Jesus challenged the disciples to leave also, Peter's answer was, "Lord we are connected to you through a God given relationship. How can we leave?"

The best relationships in the world for us are the ones we don't try to find and the ones we are not trying to keep. Each day is a journey to our destiny! Our spiritual father is a part of the process for us to reach our God given destiny.

Don't resist when God connects and when He chooses your spiritual father. God looks and sees your eternal destiny. His connections are not always the ones we would make or choose.

Often they are cross-cultural, cross-denominational, cross-geographical, cross-gender and age. Don't try and rationalize who you think it should be. Don't try and make the decision for God. God has connected us for **His** Glory!

Connection +Adding = Building

And they said, "Come, let us build ourselves a city" (Genesis 11:4).

The agreement they made between themselves gave them such power that they were able to build a city. As the people connected they became one with each other.

The connection gave them the ability to build. We cannot expect to build the pattern of heaven unless we connect as heaven is connected.

This new shift in the Spirit is no longer to build a new denomination, movement or club. We must network together, and allow the kingdom to invade every system and structure within our cities to make His name famous.

It is this connection; these relationships and in particular the relationship of that of a spiritual father which provides us with the power to build a pathway from the natural to the supernatural.

While Adam and Eve stayed connected and worked together, they had dominion and a pathway to God. *"Adam walked with God in the cool of the day."*

This is why so many churches today are dead! They are no longer walking in agreement with each other or building on relationships divinely appointed by God. Churches are condemning the relationship of spiritual fathering. They compare it to a religious ritual undertaken by some religious movements, rather than allowing the Lord to give them the understanding and revelation of the concept. It prevents them from walking in a powerful model that will impart and cause an inheritance to be granted to our nations and to be passed down to the generations to come.

...they were all with one accord... (Acts 2:1).

They were in agreement together, connecting together. We have tried to copy Pentecost and the early church by Fasting for 40 days. (We nearly killed ourselves, and Jenny Craig and weight watchers went broke!)

We tried to sell everything (a good way to become poor).

We had house-to-house communion (no housework was achieved and marriages suffered).

But we missed the vital key–**agreement and connection**.

In the book of Acts they were declaring and praying the WORD and WILL of God, they were all in agreement. They were all connected to one another. They had spent forty days together, and today, after three, we'd be leaving THAT church!

We are so desperate for revival, and so busy trying to bring it. WHY? The essence of our desire is pride. When we look, none of us can relate one to another. Pentecostals won't work with the Charismatics. None of them are good enough for the word of faith stream; and who wants to work with the apostolics?

Could pride really be the issue here? We want our "church" to have it, to have built it, to keep it and for others to come and try and get it.

Yet God has given every stream and river and denomination a revelation. Just imagine if we connected together, relating, and working with our hands joined together.

What is connecting? It is as it says in Ephesians, the perfecting and completeness of the Body of Christ. God wants the Body of

Christ to connect, to be perfected. Why?

So we will produce life and have a heritage to pass on to the next generation. We can then cry in one voice, "Come Lord Jesus, Come."

Chapter Two

A Son Is a Builder of the Family Home

By January 2000, I was jaded with what I had seen so far in the Body of Christ, and especially the church. Like most of us, I too sung the songs like "God is building His church" and had gone home wondering, well then, If God is building His church, somewhere in the past 2,000 years something has gone wrong.

God had not kept up with the times and this so-called building was a sham. I often wondered if we would go home Sunday and come back the next weekend and find "old sister Bertha" dead in her pew, and no one having a clue. This wasn't relationship, this was a staged Hollywood production where musicians were fighting for the next "Dove" award. Businessmen wanting to be the next Ziggy Ziggler, and pastors counting how many platforms had opened up for them. By now you may be slowly agreeing, or if you're honest, I have touched a nerve and have steam exuding from ears and nose in anger.

It was at this stage in my life that I remember lying prostrate on my living room floor, crying out to God for something new, that a scripture opened up as never before.

...from whom the whole family in heaven and earth is named... (Ephesians 3:15).

What's this, I asked over and over? Family is where I find a relationship, a place of safety and where I give my life in covenant. Was there such a place, or greater still, such a people on the face of the earth? More importantly, what was this family? So my search began...

> *What house will you build for Me?* (Acts 7:49).

> *Could you build a dwelling place for me?* (New Living Trans.)

A son sees a home, his place of birth, his name, his residence and his family. He sees security, protection and love. A person who joins and just becomes a church member, looks at the church and sees a church building. They see meetings as the means to an end, they enjoy fellowship and friendship but rarely do they have a revelation of relationship. This is why the church has not progressed; believing the platform and the pulpit was the church. God, forgive us! If we go back to the first church in Acts 2, and I am aware of all the faults while it was in the birthing stages which we will discuss in a later chapter, we see that the platform was NOT the place of relationship—the home was.

In our home, the inner sanctum is our living room, the dinner table, and, if like me you have daughters, then the bathroom is the place where we grow, laugh and most of all relate and display love.

A pastor said to me a few weeks ago that the platform was where relationships were built.

How sad! How from a platform can we communicate our heart to each son separately? Could this be the reason that the church has become an institution that no longer relates to society and has insulated her from the outside? If we can't even talk to those who we are in covenant with, how do we relate to a dying loveless world?

Those in covenant can never isolate themselves. Pastors, don't fool yourselves, if you isolate yourself from your people and only stay where it is safe, then may I suggest you have a wonderful paddock full of sheep, but you do not have a home full of sons.

Who gives "Birth to Whom"?

It is important to realize here that the father is the originator of the relationship and so the responsibility for the relationship is not the sons BUT the spiritual fathers.

> *...he will turn the hearts of the fathers to the children, and the hearts of the children to their fathers...* (Malachi 4:6).

The heart of the father must turn to the sons first. It is NOT sons looking for fathers; it isn't in the natural, nor is it in the spiritual. The Father sent His Son, He knew us, found us and we became His son. It is totally unscriptural to say, "I found the Father." He was neither lost nor were you out there trying to find Him. He saw and heard your deep desire and made Himself known to you.

The spiritual father, just as the heavenly Father, must initiate the relationship by first recognizing that the son is in fact his own and then accept the son into his family. By doing this, he allows honor and accountability into the nature of the son and closes the door on any insecurity. At the same time, the father must remember this is a spiritual dynamic and not a natural one. He must be careful that he never allows the son to become emotionally dependent or manipulate him. Fathers must constantly reach out to their sons, search out the relationship to bring security to the connection. If this does not happen, then insecurity breeds, bringing with it the seeds of rejection and discord.

No relationship should ever have an element of manipulation in it, it can be tempting but it will lead to destruction. In Acts 1:16-20 we see where Judas tried to build a relationship by manipulation and his gain led to a place of death.

Galatians 4:1-5. Paul elaborates here that although we can be an heir to all, if there's no revelation, we can be as slaves having guardians over us. The church today is in transition. Few walk in their true inheritance and few understand the total concept of heritage. In verse 2, we see there is an "appointed time by the father". This is a small 'f'; or in other words, the appointed time for a son is not in the time totally of the heavenly Father, He just places the cry in a son's heart to be adopted. If spiritual fathers don't have an ability to define accuracy in their spiritual walk, they will either never really understand the concept of apostolic fathering, or try to gain too many sons out of their appointed time and this could lead to disaster.

Building... it's the Passion of any Son

A son will always think, "How will the house benefit? How can I improve the "building" of the home as a family unit? How can I help to construct and to establish the foundation of the church? (House)"

A son wants to be involved in the home; he is interested in every aspect of the "house" and the dynamic of it.

...for I always do those things that please Him (John 8:29).

A son's heart always wants to promote the house, the family, and the father of the house. His heart is always to do that which is pleasing to the father and to the family as a whole. A son will see the full picture of the family; he will also see the relationships within the family and the continuing process that these go through. A son will always be watching the condition of the "house"; he sees its internal and external state. A healthy and clean home is important to a son.

Sons have a different mindset. Their paradigm underwent a total transformation in the process of becoming a son. This caused their perception of church to be different from that of a member. A son has progressed from the concept of blessing, to a genre of building, realizing it's not just about receiving blessing and blessing people, but he is there to build into the people, into the living stones of the temple of God.

Sons are building toward prophetic destiny and so will harness their impatience and remember that destiny is their long- term goal and that destiny is a daily walk, not an instant commodity.

Sons Build the Family Name

Not only does a son build the house internally and externally, but is also a builder of the family name. The name of the church is important to him. In a natural family, the name of the family speaks of the family's nature, character, reputation and integrity. For a son is a builder and wants to build the name of his family well.

Often in natural families there tends to be a "language" that is spoken by the family. It will have a particular language that the father of the house and those connected to him will speak. Outsiders may not understand the language until they are connected to the house itself. In the transition to connection we must be careful this does not become off putting and a source of isolation.

When Jesus declared the Name of His Father, He knew that within the name the whole character of His Father was declared. Sons know that when they also declare the name of the father or the house (family), this allows him stature before God and men. It brings him to a place of standing that will connect the son to relationships with others of God's sons. When Moses laid hands on Joshua, this gave Joshua a stature before God and men; therefore the son now has the same stature as the spiritual father, on earth and in the heavenlies.

...I have declared to them your name... (John 17:26).

A son knows that his father's reputation becomes his. The same respect his father has with men, the son has also. As people and ministers accept his father, the son is also accepted and respected. Joshua had the same respect Moses had, because he was his spiritual son. A son knows he doesn't have to strive for people to see him the way they see his father. What his father walks in the son will automatically walk into.

Sons Build and Further Their Father's Purpose

Samuel so affected the life of David, that his fundamental vision, when he became the king of Israel, was to bring the ark of God back to Israel. Samuel's passion was that the ark be returned to his beloved nation. If we look from the time he was a young boy, he ministered before the ark in the temple with Eli. This was the reason he was consecrated for service in his mother's womb.

Historical records say that David, when he was on the run from Saul, spent ten years with Samuel. Here he not only learnt how to rule with a kingdom governmental authority, but there was an impartation and transfer of prophetic destiny, personal and national. David's ability to join his heart to Samuel for an eternal purpose caused spiritual succession and the furtherance of God's eternal plans and purposes.

Is This Concept Really of God?

It is so heartbreaking that those with no revelation of spiritual fathering criticize the concept, and believe it to have come from a religious system with no power in it at all.

Sadly they have taken one passage of Scripture where Jesus said, *"Call no man father upon the earth."* We could now take this to the extreme and believe that we should not call our natural father, "father" either, for Jesus did say upon the earth! Perhaps it would be wiser to distinguish what Jesus was really saying in this passage and not build a doctrine out of one verse to disprove a theory we don't like or understand.

The word is also used in the context of our heavenly Father 258 times, and our earthly fathers 140 times. It is also used in the context of Abraham, the father of our faith. This word is also the same word used when Paul said in Corinthians, *"Where are the fathers?"* So what was Jesus condemning? In Matthew 23:9, Jesus had been talking to the Pharisees, and further study of the Greek, finds the word **father there is** *pater,* which means **founder of a race** or in this case, **founder of Christianity.** Members of the Sanhedrin called themselves fathers, using it in this context (Acts 7:2; 22:1). History tells us the Sanhedrin "fathers" were the hypocrites as the Sanhedrin "lorded" it over the people solely because of their religious position and power. How sad we threw the baby out with the bath-water and therefore disqualified ourselves from walking in an incredible revelation.

Case Studies

Not long ago I was speaking to a young woman who thought she had met her spiritual father. The relationship developed and the woman moved her family to the nation her newfound relationship was in. Suddenly there was trouble within her marriage. They were a young married couple with very small children, and her husband became exceedingly disturbed by the new relationship that was budding. The woman's spiritual father had been calling her when her husband was not home, discussing private marital situations Of course, it caused discord to come into the marriage. After a time it was obvious that an emotional dependency had started and the woman woke up to what was happening! The sad end to this story was that this had now caused so much unhappiness and mistrust between her and her husband that the marriage was anything but happy.

This situation is not a one off as we are seeing it over and over in the Body of Christ. This is the very thing that by revealing apostolic fathering, we will hopefully eradicate the messes that our lack of knowledge has caused.

Another situation that was brought to light not long ago was the story of a young, single mum. When I met her she was defensive and I knew something had happened. After searching deeper into her life, I found the most disturbing situation had occurred that I had ever come across. Her pastor had come to her and said that a gentleman in the church was now to be her spiritual father. The relationship with this other man developed until soon it was now becoming out of hand. He called daily and would visit in her home causing her to feel vulnerable and uncomfortable. Soon the gentleman wanted to take the relationship further. In the beginning it was just a fatherly hug until before long it became a deeper embrace!

Shocking as these situations are, the fact is they are true and both women are now in a position where they will not trust men in authority again. This is appalling and if pastors do not have the revelation and knowledge of fathering, then it is advisable not to institute it into their churches just yet.

Another situation was where a pastor was in the process of transitioning his church from members to sons. A young man became disturbed, as week after week, the pastor would declare from the pulpit "If you leave my church, you will miss it, and therefore be out of God's hand of protection." The young man soon became distraught, as for reasons beyond his control he had to leave the district and his church. He felt he had missed "it" and every time some situation occurred in his life that caused pain he was convinced he was now out of God's protective covering. We had to talk to him and find out what was exactly the "it" he would be missing. He had no clue but knew "it" was preached week after week! This situation was really a form of control and manipulation by the pastor.

God is bigger than most of us think or believe and he is capable of protecting us so we do not miss "it"! It is unfair to put this pressure on our members or our sons. God is bigger than any pastor or church, so to assume that if people leave "our church" they walk away from God and their destiny, is placing yourself in a place of superiority!

Chapter Three

The Fruit of the House: Sons

The hardest dynamic to accept in this new apostolic move, is the fact we are now moving toward corporate destiny and away from individual ministry. For a number of years, I had a growing itinerant ministry and when I came into an apostolic network, I had to see further than I had ever seen before. This was no longer about a personal ministry but about corporate destiny! My ministry was no longer important, but building His Kingdom was the ultimate vision. What a paradigm shift! We talk about corporate blessing in the charismatic church and also about body ministry, but this dynamic is deeper than this teaching. This dynamic touches the very core of our destinies where they soon become entwined together. It goes even beyond my destiny just being entwined with the Spiritual fathers but as brothers, we now relate together with one vision, one call and one ultimate goal, and now the family's destiny is entwined together.

But the children (sons)... (Exodus 1:7).

We see it was not one son that caused the nation to increase abundantly, multiply and grow exceedingly, but the sons! So it is with this new generation, no longer one man with a platform ministry but we will see the true fruit of Apostolic fathering... **brothers connecting** to bring about prophetic national destiny!

In Exodus 2, we see a group of women who understood the prophetic destiny of their nation, and knew a deliverer would soon come. At that time, could it be that only one mother tried to save her child? I think it would be foolish to think this way as the feelings of a parent, even in the animal kingdom, go beyond even the fear of death itself. These women connected together and allowed an accuracy to come to them. They found the correct baby, the deliverer, and the one who would fulfill prophetic destiny. They defied all they knew and Pharaoh himself to change the face of a nation!

Understanding Connection

What is this connectivity that can cause us to walk into this new dynamic and take our nation with us?

John 14:20-21 says, *...you will know that I am in My Father, and you are in Me, and I in you. He who has My commandments and keeps them, it is he who loves Me. And he who loves Me, will be loved by My Father, and I will love him and manifest Myself to him.*

When there is a victory, a son rejoices with the father and the family, but when there is a storm, sons will feel the burden of it.

In Matthew 14: 22-31, the disciples were given an instruction by Jesus *"to go to the other side."* Suddenly a horrendous storm front comes in and an encounter with the forces of nature takes them all by surprise. While in their boat, the twelve see Jesus walking on the water. They call out in fear thinking it is a ghost. Jesus, calming their fears, cries out *"It is I"*. Now remember, when Jesus said it is *"I"*, the word 'I', held the same power and authority as the Great I Am, the Creator of the Universe.

Peter answers Jesus and said, *"If it's You, tell me to come"* Jesus said, *"Come."* Jesus had no option but to say come. If He hadn't, He would have lied, as He was 'He'. How often we say, "oh Jesus, if it (a new job etc.) is really you, then let this or that happen" and when it does happen, we are happy. We are now sure it is the Lord, but often not so happy with the consequences.

Though the sea was high and the waves lapping at his sides hitting his face, Peter came to the call of his Master. Peter gets out of the boat and walks toward Jesus ignoring his Master's first instruction. The other eleven were left in the boat bailing out water for their lives, so as to fight the storm. Peter on the other hand, chose an experience over corporate destiny. Where did Jesus take Peter? Was it over the other side? NO, they went straight back into the boat and back into corporate life.

A son cannot try to walk alone with his father. He must acknowledge that corporate means brothers and we are working together for the purpose of corporate destiny; no one gets an encounter outside corporate life above another. During the storm the son may need to hear the calming voice of the father of the house, but once he hears, he will weather the storm, and continue with the other sons in the house to fulfil the vision of the house.

It is amazing when you look at Peter's life. Whilst everyone was leaving Jesus, Jesus said "OK boys, why don't you lot take off as well." It was Peter the one we don't often talk about in this way, (it is usually John we see as being the son,) who said, *"Where can we go? You have the words that bring us life!"* At that time Peter's whole life was about to be affected, his reputation, and his own personal agenda. It would have been easier for Peter to say, *"This is way too hard, I'm off"*, but he led the way, and said he wanted to follow, which then allowed the others to do the same.

Here we see the true heart of a son. When everyone is leaving, criticizing and speaking ill of the father of the house, a true son will say, "Where else can I go, you have the words that speak and impart life to me."

When talking about spiritual sons, we also must look at the relationship the son has with the father. When a son sees someone touch his father's integrity, honor or character, then it becomes personal for the son! A true son is always loyal; if you don't like his father then you don't like him!

He who hates Me, hates My Father also (John 15:23).

When a son sees someone touch his father, it becomes personal. A son will not have a relationship or build with someone who can't or won't build or be on relational terms with his father. We see this when an overexcited Peter cut off the ear of a soldier! A son isn't interested in building his ministry, he wants to build the Kingdom, and to build the Kingdom means he is building the family. Just as Jesus, God's Son worked to bring the glory and acknowledgment to His father, so it is with a spiritual son; he is committed to the end to his family.

And whatever you ask in My name, that will I do, that the Father may be glorified in the Son (John 14:13).

A son's work is not to build his own name and agenda but to bring Glory to the father. At the end of the day this is the sign of a true son, "his" work brings glory not to himself but to his father.

Sons Cover Sin; Hirelings Will Do All to Expose.

A son will always, out of respect, cover his father's nakedness.

A hireling loves to expose the flesh and the weaknesses of leadership. They gossip in the guise of saying it is "counsel" or saying they are praying and asking you too, but in reality they see any weakness of the flesh, discover and then expose it.

In Genesis 9:20-25, we read that Noah's drinking as far as we know, was an incident; it was a one off affair. Ham, Noah's son, saw his father's nakedness and gossiped by telling his other brothers, Shem and Japheth. Shem and Japheth took a garment, and placed it on their shoulders.

The garment represented a covering, a mantle. It covered that which was negative about their father and replaced it with a positive cover.

The covering we could say, could be that of a good report. (It is better to speak words of life and words that protect rather than negative words and words that lay a person bare and exposed to hurt.)

They lay the coat first on **both their** shoulders. One didn't just carry the coat, but both brothers took it as though they were one. This speaks of connection; these two young men stood together in agreement and as they approached their father they were one together. These two young men were granted a spiritual blessing and prosperity for them and their descendants to walk into.

To do such an act, symbolizes their strength and support to their father; the mantle represents government. They took on the leadership of the family for the moment their father was unable to because of his weakness. It is amazing to perceive that neither of these young men had a problem with pride; it seems they walked in humility, placing their father's reputation before their own.

The two sons, Shem and Japheth, walked backwards toward their father in an act of honor and respect so their eyes could not see their father's weakness. We can only wonder if the story of the fall of their descendants, Adam and Eve, had been passed down to them. If they had been told that the fall occurred, not only because they were deceived with words, but, because Eve had looked upon the fruit, and once she saw it, sin became inevitable. Of course, once they had handled sin, then the Presence of God their Father, would no longer be theirs to walk in. It seemed these boys knew how easy it would be to lose the presence of the father, just as Adam had done!

Noah then said to Ham in Genesis 9:25, *"a servant of servants he shall be to his brethren."*

Ham lost the spirit of sonship. The prodigal son never lost the spirit of sonship. Why? He touched the inheritance and not the father. To expose the father and touch him invokes a curse that should not be taken lightly. It is a serious thing to dishonor a father.

Honor your father and mother... that it may be well with you and you may live long on the earth (Ephesians 6:2-3).

This promise can be about natural and spiritual fathers and sons. Obedience to a spiritual father is a son's obligation; a rebel risks his life spiritually and naturally. A son should not connect to an apostolic spiritual father without serious consideration.

To date we have had many pastors call themselves fathers without revelation of what a true father is; that is why Paul said we have so many instructors but so few fathers. To be a father is an **apostolic** function. Therefore, when we have pastors try and fulfill his function, it will fail and also when we have women who want to be the Mother of all Israel, we again, have disorder. Anyone can be fatherly but true apostolic order is where the apostle is a spiritual father.

Sons cover the nakedness of a father, not a cover up but be a covering. To cover is to shield an area until things can be dealt with properly and the problem solved. It would be unwise for any to ignore problems in the character of a father and allow him to fall. We have seen this in the past where unwisely it was a silent ethical code to leave sin and grave character flaws unchecked. Apostolic men fell and sons were left hurt and wounded.

Diverse Sons

When we look at Peter, a son can take heart. Just before Jesus, whom, let's say was Peter's spiritual father, was crucified, Peter denied Him. Peter had to deal with the devastation he felt about himself. After the resurrection he stands up, and takes on the role of leadership even when his heart and his mind were condemning him! Possibly the most healing words he heard was when Jesus said to him *"Follow Me."* After all that Peter did in denying his Beloved Lord, Jesus never brought up his past but appreciated Peter for what he was now, today. The most healing words to a son, after he feels he has blown it and could be rejected by his father, the one he is committed to, are the words of forgiveness and trust.

We should note here that a son's past must never be brought up to bring condemnation. We find no scripture to back that up but in fact the opposite, and there must be no condemnation. The past must only be discussed so as to give accuracy to certain behavior patterns in the son's life for the future. Discuss it and allow the son to move on, never keep bringing up the act as this then shows a character flaw within the father. Fathers get sons passed sin consciousness and teach them to walk in light and life; forward into destiny not backward into failure.

Just after the resurrection, they were casting lots to see who would be the next disciple. Matthias was chosen and Joseph was rejected. What an awful moment for Joseph! He was the one with the superior qualifications, but still lost out to another. This is the moment that every son will have to cope with at some time. He is serving as best he can, perhaps longer than the rest, yet another is chosen. A son in this position can die with a spirit of rejection if he is allowed to. If the father allows a spirit of rejection to come into his soul, it will kill the dimensions of the spirit that have been opened for him, because he is a son. A son must realize if he is not chosen, it is because it is not yet his time, but his time will eventually come. He must know he is not serving because he has a position or a title, but because he is a son.

Imagine how each son felt that day; Joseph must have had to deal with the feelings of rejection and hurt. Matthias rejoiced! And Peter, have we ever cast a thought how he felt, standing up taking the leadership role in front of Mary, the mother of Jesus, and the brothers of Jesus? Not many days before he had denied and rejected Mary's son, and Jesus' own brothers.

In 3 John: 9-10, John was writing to the church and said that Diotrephes did not want to receive apostolic men or their input, nor did he relate in a healthy wholesome way and this would result in exposing him when he came.

Strife causes teams to split and turn sour, causing the work and dynamic of the house to be affected and relationships to be severed. Maturity will see this happening and in a loving way minister to all, so the team stays intact. It is rare that any situation can not be resolved.

If it is allowed to continue, a relationship will reach the point where little can be salvaged and friends become enemies. In a healthy, mature house this should never reach such a point!

How Does a Son Cope with a Judas in the House?

A Judas of course hurts the father, but we often forget that a Judas in the house can cause great pain for the sons also. When a Judas betrays the house, we have to learn how to deal with those who hurt us, and the house. Peter is the picture of a mature son in how he handled the situation. He stands up and says Judas has gone, now let's fill the gap, not looking at history, but focusing on destiny. We must be so careful not to wallow in self-pity and unforgiveness, but close the chapter on yesterday, forgive and go on.

Forgiving prevents another from exerting control.

Just as a father has to let him go, a son does also, and not let the dead determine the destiny of the living. We can make the mistake of dwelling on the betrayal and become bitter but this will then lead to a victim mentality, and soon the dynamic of a **victim** and not a **victor,** contaminates and infects the house.

If this dynamic is allowed to go on, it will cause a negative effect on the very nature of the house and the younger sons in process.

It is important that we never let the negative be our starting point. It is important that all be given a positive starting point.

Pastors who have been previously hurt in this way will only give an artificial starting point. Grace is not artificial; it is pure, whole and positive and the very mark of an Apostolic Father. Grace was always the point that Jesus gave to each person who'd sinned as a new start.

Many pastors today are saying that with every twelve leaders we will have one Judas, and this causes fear and apprehension. It is better to say that for every Judas in the house, there was a Jesus for him to follow and then allow grace to be the covering for him to change. Jesus never chose to reject Judas, He gave Judas three and a half years to change.

How Does a Son React and Cope When There is an Absalom in the House?

Absalom was the third son of David; he was perfect in physical appearance, eloquent and dignified. How does a son react to him in the first place? You would think a son would be extremely jealous of him, but the Word tells us he had a way of conniving and manipulating the people into following him. We know that as wonderful as Absalom seemed on the outside, deep down he was a murderous, treacherous, godless and conceited man. He murdered his own brother, betrayed his father and died in vanity! (2 Samuel 13:28-39).

Absalom had his brother Amon killed to avenge the man who had sinned against his sister. David grieved the death of his son and when Absalom found out his father was aware of his act, fled to his grandfather. David's grief was deep and as the Word says, *"the soul of King David longed to go forth to Absalom."* He then looked for him. It would have been better for David and Absalom to leave Absalom with his grandfather. The story may have been different and many lives saved in the process.

A father has to use wisdom with his son, when to leave all and regain him (parable of the lost sheep). When do I wait at my door constantly praying and looking, (parable of the prodigal son) and, when do I leave a son where he and the rest of the father's sons are safe?

Absalom was a son with a treacherous agenda; the Word says, *"he stole the hearts of the men of Israel"*. A father must discern a son's agenda for his family's sake! Remember, only a father who is secure in his walk and call can ever truly discern with a pure heart (2 Samuel 14:32).

David only partially forgave Absalom. He confessed he would forgive him but would not see him. This is not forgiveness and what David hoped to achieve we will never know. All he gained through his own stubbornness was a miserable life. His attitude estranged his son from him permanently and eventually caused him the greatest heartache a parent can ever know.

Every spiritual father must look at his inner most feelings toward his son, and ask himself, "Why am I reacting to my son the way I am? Am I reacting to a quality that is in my son that I know is within me and don't like and have well hidden?"

Every spiritual father must be on the alert for a son like Absalom who is rebellious and out to cause rebellion in the house! Sons must also be so careful that they are not used as lure into another son's deceitful behavior.

Here are the steps that were Absalom's downfall that can lead to strife and rebellion within a family. These are the characteristics of disloyalty. Every son must be vigilant not to be enticed into rebellion in the house.

1) Maneuvered for recognition within the house.

2) Maneuvered for the praise of the people.

3) He began to have spiritual pride, (have revelations beyond the father of the house.)

4) Questioned authority and spiritual insight.

5) Had a critical spirit, questioned decisions being made about money etc.

6) He was competitive and made comparisons.

7) Drew people to himself.

8) Sowed seeds of bitterness. He needed to have people see him and have their eyes on him.

9) No longer wanted to uplift the King but discredit him, in other words his agenda became political and no longer Kingdom.

When an Absalom is discovered, a son must also cut him off, just as the father must sever him from the house. If a son doesn't cut him off, then the same spirit of rebellion will affect and taint him also. There can be no mercy to a rebellious and unrepentant Absalom in the house, although Father God will always extend His hand of love and Grace to a rebellious son who will repent.

WARNING: The House is going through Negative Times!

A son must be careful not to pick up the negative habits or message of the house, especially if the house is going through a period of shaking. In this case we must always realize, although in covenant with the father of the house, we still must find a way to restore the relationship, and not live to find retribution.

Remember that internal problems can sap away at the spiritual energy within a house and slow forward momentum.

The motto of a mature father will always be **"Don't ignore, restore!"**

> *...the lamp of God had not yet gone out... in the temple (house)... where the ark of God was* (1 Samuel 3:3).

Eli the priest, the father of Hophni and Phinehas, had allowed the light to dim in the temple. With no light in the temple, the behavior of Eli's sons reflected the attitude and message of the house; darkness. Their behavior then brought not only dishonor to the house and their father, but brought themselves and their descendants into slavery. These two sons Hopni and Phinehas eventually lost the spirit of sonship, and, just as Ham, Noah's son, did they became slaves.

> *...everyone who is left in your house, (all your descendants) will come and bow down to him (My faithful priest) and beg for food and money* (I Samuel 2:36). (Paraphrased)

In (1 Samuel 1:28; 2:18,19) Hannah gave her son to the prophet. The mantle, the call and the priesthood, (i.e. the inheritance which had belonged to Eli's two sons) fell onto Samuel, the spiritual son. His mother covered him with the mantle she herself had made him for a time till he reached manhood, and then she had to hand him to the prophet to look after.

A warning to young sons! Samuel followed Eli so closely that he also picked up on Eli's weaknesses. His own sons became wayward and were a source of concern for Samuel.

We must be careful to always reflect the positive message of the house and not pick up and reflect the weaknesses of it. When a house is going through hard times, focus on the positive side. When there is gossip in the house, it can be tempting to become involved in the negative talk within. It is at this time to determine not to be involved.

When a house goes through a time of financial and emotional adversity, keep focused on the Word of God, and make sure your relationship with the Lord is pure and unpolluted by any outside sources.

We must make sure we are hungering after more of the Lord. Psalm 63:8 *"My soul chases and follows hard after you."* Always maintain a fervent hunger and thirst for the Lord. It is particularly at this time that we must stir passion and become lovers of Him.

No matter what the house is going through and no matter what the relationship is to the father of the house, we must keep our relationship with Jesus close. Pant for Him, and never allow a cold or lukewarm heart to develop.

A father must never allow a son to rely on his spiritual father's relationship with the Lord; he must learn to break through into a new level and dimension for himself daily, to develop his own relationship with the Lord. Sadly, an insecure father keeps a son reliant on his (the father's) relationship with the Lord, and this can keep sons in a cycle of dependence.

The people cried to Samuel to give them a king because of their individual difficulties in establishing their own personal relationship with God. They continually wanted something external to substantiate what the prophets were telling them.

Saul reigned as a king and David served as a son. The Scriptures say that of David's descendants, there was always one on the throne. Sons bring forth descendants... the next generation... Sons leave a legacy.

After Saul was appointed king, Samuel said to Israel that now they would have to live by regulations and laws. Their dependence would be on the man they chose to rule and regulate their nation.

We must never allow anyone to put us in the position of a king. It is so easy because when we are king, many are dependent upon us. This mindset is one born out of insecurity and dependence. The choice is ours. We will always have people who like to make us feel like a king because people like being kings and like having kings. God's way is obedience to Him, and serving as a son.

Look at the Israelites at the time of Moses. Moses was on the mountain in the presence of God, and the Israelites and Aaron are in the valley wanting to worship something tangible, a golden calf. If not careful, we too can also be looking for some new manifestation to help us worship God, instead of developing our own individual relationship.

There is nothing wrong with a manifestation but when we chase the manifestation and not the one who brings it, we are in danger of being in error.

...they turned aside after dishonest gain (1 Samuel 8:3).

It was Samuel's **son's** behavior that caused a whole nation to cry out for a king to judge them and not the prophet. The regretful behavior of a son reflecting the behavior of the house caused the whole nation to stray. It is a fearful thing that a son's behavior, good or bad, can affect the destiny of not just his family or church, but also his city and nation (1 Samuel 8:10-19).

Before the day the nation cried out for a king, it had always been ruled by a judge. Now they no longer wanted to be moderated by a man of God's choosing, but by a man of theirs.

The nation broke the father and son order God had in place up until then. No longer did the government of God flow down from father to son. They lost the spirit of sonship and the nation became servants.

This will be the behavior of the king who will reign over you: He will take your sons... and appoint them to his servant (vs. 11-14).

When there is no father/son order, people revert back to the flesh and churches revert back to programs.

Perhaps the reason we have seen the church almost decline into a business where programs, money and numbers have become the priority, is because we have lost the father/son order. No longer are pastors raising sons and building a heritage to pass down. They are gathering members who have given him a title, respecting the title more than the man.

God has not changed. He still has this order and pattern in place. We look at the early church and often try as many different programs as we can to follow the pattern, but we are forgetting one thing; the early church was based on father/son order. Look at Corinthians; Paul asks where the fathers are. In the books of Titus and Timothy, Paul addresses both men as his sons before establishing order in the church.

My Members Are Leaving... Help!

A compromising church is one that does not set boundaries. It allows undisciplined behavior, it is a fatherless church. Undisciplined people are drawn to fatherless churches. If you want to shake your church, announce you are the father of the house and teach about sonship–watch the members scatter!

Not long ago I was invited to a church in Germany for four days. My message was connection and establishing correct order. The church had been built on the concept of membership and it was our desire to reposition the church into a "house" where sons were connected to the father of the house and to each other, instead of just being attending members.

There were a number of women in this church doing their own thing. They had their own little "intercessory" prayer groups, attended the church when they felt the need, but were definitely not connected. Many became enraged as correction and order came, feeling that their agenda had been touched. Some repented that weekend and connected into the house. Not long after, I heard from the pastor that all the lone rangers had left and the pastor was now feeling very grieved at the loss.

When we start to bring order into the house, those who have their own agenda and the spirit of a hireling will never stay. This was not a loss but a revealing of the heart of his people!

There is a huge difference between losing sons and losing individualists; a hireling will leave because he can never stay in a house where there is the pattern and order of heaven.

Fathers, Look Before You Leap... Don't Go to Heaven with a Millstone!

If a son leaves, no matter how hurt and broken the father feels, the fruit of a mature father is to have a passion to restore, not ignore the broken relationship. It is a general rule that a relationship that is not restored will keep deteriorating and it is not to be left to a son to restore it because, *"the hearts of the fathers **must** turn to their sons."*

When people leave at various times in the life of a house, perhaps through a storm, shaking, transition etc. we must be cautious as an insecure father will see it as a personal affront.

When people leave the church, always try to restore the relationship so there is no animosity. A mark of maturity is a man/woman who can forgive and release.

In Matthew 6:14, Jesus told us that we are to forgive, if we hold offense our Father in heaven holds us to account.

A father is to be mature, that is the reason he is a father. Therefore, in that maturity he is to forgive and restore first, even when it seems he is the one who has been hurt the most!

Matthew 18:5-6, again speaks on fathering. Jesus says, *"One who receives a child (even spiritual) and then causes the son to sin, would be better off drowning."*

Spiritual fathering and walking in the apostolic is a huge responsibility. Perhaps it is better to think twice before jumping in.

If there is a problem between a father and son, a mature father does not find a third party to agree with him. He goes to his son, and like Jesus, washes his feet humbly and with tears of restoration.

What natural father throws his son out of the house and severs the relationship? No, a good father turns his heart toward the son, wanting to see him fulfill his destiny.

Perhaps this issue is one we must look at with serious reflection. We are seeing fathers beget sons and disunite from them as soon as there is discontent in the relationship. Let's be somber and ask ourselves seriously, "Is this really God?"

When a son leaves a church, pastors often give the impression that all fellowship should be cut off. This is a knee jerk reaction and should never happen in a family. Relationships should never be based on behavior or giving people a rating on performance; they must have a foundation on covenant.

What sort of message do we give the world if we are no better than they themselves? Hurt us and we cut you off!

This is Mafia; Not Family!

Fathers, if you are not mature, do not try and walk into a function that needs above all else, a mature, humble character. Immature fathers will cause a continuum of immaturity and hurt to grow in the system. It is often unseen until trouble strikes, and will invariably be seen in the next generation.

God created man and woman. When they sinned and had to leave the garden, God didn't disconnect man from fellowship; He continued to speak to him for hundreds of years. Why? God created a team, man and woman. No matter how they perform, teams stay connected; it is through **relationship** that they connect, not **performance**.

When performance and behavior becomes the foundation of the team, we will find that when they fail to meet the standards we set them, the relationship itself will be severed.

We must NOT delude ourselves, this is not fathering!

Chapter Four

A Father Brings His Sons Their Inheritance.

Sadly, many of us have been in a church that we embraced as our family only to find that we were soon being reduced to all our wrongs.

Today, as I minister in the Body of Christ, I see so many Christians and ministers who are hurt, bitter, angry and frustrated, because they connected to what they thought was an apostolic father and found that all the life and purpose of God was sucked out of them. I empathize with those of you who are there now, but as you read this chapter I pray that your eyes will be opened and you see that beyond the pain there is hope, purpose, destiny, future, and most of all life for you.

If I could give you a word it would be the one God gave me when I sat in the same seat you now find yourself in, "Don't give up!"

For the past 2,000 years, we have waited with expectancy for the "next new move," the next revival etc. Today, there is a breaking forth of men and women of God who are bringing the relevance of God's Word and aligning it with God's present activity on the earth today.

These men and women with apostolic natures have the ability to cry out and say, "This is that!"

For 2,000 years there has been a constant flow of fresh outpouring, but we are at the place in history where we will no longer have another outpouring, but rather a consummation of all He has poured out in the past millenniums. There will be an extraordinary demonstration of the power of the Holy Spirit, as every move and every revival meets and creates a culmination like we have never seen previously. What will we call this move? **The apostolic!** We will see the healing revival link up to the word of faith etc. and mantles upon mantles that men and women have walked in over the years, suddenly connect into the greatest outpouring ever. You, who are downcast, gird up your loins, have faith in God and run, declaring, "I hear the sound of an **abundance** of rain."

How I hunger to see these true apostles appear, men who teach the truth and present it in such a way that we see God. Men who are so connected to God that they have the ability to form His kingdom, life and nature in us, so we can represent not just another religious order but His will, His plans and His prophetic destiny in the cities and nations where we live.

Paul cried in Galatians 4:19, *"My little children (my sons) for whom I labor in birth again until Christ (His nature, character, destiny and purpose) is formed in you."*

This is the cry from the heart of a true apostle. A father's purpose on this earth is to form kingdom-life and nature into every son God gives him. Men, who birth God's plans into their sons and whose deepest desire is to see their sons not only walk in, but **be** the fulfillment and finishing of their desire.

I pray, that on reading the last paragraph, it has stirred in you a passion and cry and that now you have decided to leave the past and its hurts where they belong, in the annals of history, and walk into your prophetic destiny.

Fathers lock Sons into Their Divine Inheritance

So now brethren I commend you to God and to the word of His grace, which is able to build you up and give you an inheritance among all those who are sanctified (Acts 20:32).

Apostolic fathers teach apostolic doctrine, that is, building sons up and bringing them into the inheritance due to them by their positioning as sons. Apostolic teaching fast-forwards sons into their inheritance rather than just allowing them to come into blessing.

Unless fathers teach their sons how to lock into inheritance and not just blessing, the sons will never come to a place of self government and rule in their own lives. Their lives must be a continual intake instead of controlled output. When we keep our people in a place where they continually seek blessing, we never allow them to come into a new level of faith. They will stay locked into a charismatic blessing type of mindset. It is only when we teach how to release what they already have and move into a new level of walking in their inheritance, will we bring the church into a building model, of taking from the past and accelerating it into tomorrow.

Father I want my share of your inheritance of which I am due now, instead of waiting till you die (Luke 15:12). (Paraphrased)

The prodigal only knew how to take immediate blessings from the father; he did not understand the concept of inheritance. The prodigal walked in the blessing of today, but it was not until he came home to father's character and not his belongings, did he understand the significance of the ring, the shoes and the mantle.

The prodigal son came back in an interesting way.

First he came back to his father. Then he came back to his father's house. Then he had to come back to the family and to his elder brother who was offended by the young man's behavior. Many people come back to church after a problem or an offense took them from the house. To come back to the father is a different matter altogether. If truly returning to the house, he must come back to the father of the house and make restitution.

When leaving the house, others in the family feel the hurt and loss. We are often hard on the older brother, and rightly so, as his behavior as discussed later did have flaws.

Remember, when the younger son left, his brother would have felt the loss. Not only that, the work of the house now multiplied and rested on him. Is it any wonder he was angry?

A son, in the process of returning, must come not only back to the father of the house and to the brothers, but also back to the corporate purpose and destiny of the house. Often it is easy to return to the house and the father: but to the brothers? Not so easy!

The fruits of repentance are forgiveness and restitution. Forgiveness is easy, but restitution means that not only does he go back, but must first clean up the damage left by him before reconciliation can come.

Neither party must have an attitude of "I told you so, or you'll pay." When coming back to the corporate purpose, all inner dynamics that are wrong must be cut off. Our hidden agendas, secret motives, and inner life are exposed. As we come into a new position, our heart must be sanctified. We must learn to act, NOT as a saint, but as a son.

Bring out the best robe and put it on him, and put a ring on his hand and sandals on his feet (Luke 15:22).

The robe (mantle) speaks of the father's dimension in the spirit that the son now has. The mantle was for protection and covering.

The ring represented the authority his father walked in, that now belonged to the son.

The shoes represented the father's destiny, which was now passed on to the son, they walked the same walk. This was no longer today's blessing but a walk into the destiny and purpose of God for tomorrow.

Few manage to find the gate where the father is waiting to walk in divine exchange. Many are out working in the fields, serving, believing they are in God's perfect will.

Should they have come close to their father and his character, their walk would have been one of accuracy and their destinies would be one, and they would not just enjoy today's blessing.

...for this is my son who was dead and is alive again; he was lost and is found (Luke 15:24).

These are not nice words that we have reduced to sinners being accepted "home", but the father was now calling his son into his inheritance by cutting off the past and its effects and declaring him into his destiny and inheritance.

Spiritual fathers live to build and to teach sons how to walk into an inheritance. The prodigal son wanted his portion that he had a right to, but at the wrong time. He had a short, fast rise to success, but a quick, long fall to the pigpen of defeat, failure and religion.

Today, we have so many ministers who are selfishly building their own agendas and ministries. They have no sons to pass it onto and therefore when they die, the ministry and all they built dies with them. It is heartbreaking to realize that all the generals of the past had no sons to impart to and inherit all that they had built.

It's not all about us. Should we look at the Old Testament patriarchs, we would see that it was all about the next generation.

Jesus was not here to build His ministry or His agenda but His destiny. He was here to build and connect your destiny and mine to His. Jesus was a true picture of a Father (and also the patterned Son that we will see later). All He built was not for Him but for the generations that would follow so one day they would walk in their inheritance.

A Father's Destiny Is Connected to the Destiny of His Sons

During my time here I have kept them safe; I guarded them, so that not one was lost, except Judas (John 17:12). (Paraphrased)

I am praying not only for these disciples but for all who will ever believe in Me (John 17:20). (Paraphrased)

We see this in the Old Testament patriarchs that by laying hands on their sons and speaking a blessing over them, they called them into their inheritance and connected their destinies (Genesis 49:1-4). Jacob had called his sons and prophesied their inheritance over them. He gets to Reuben and starts off in the spirit, speaking life to him, but then, because of hurt and anger getting into the flesh, it cuts him off.

Remember in Genesis 34:2, when Dinah the daughter of Jacob was raped. Jacob did not properly avenge the situation, so his sons became angry and sought revenge themselves. Simeon and Levi took their swords and killed the males of the city. Though their action was wrong, their intentions were righteous but their deed sent a message of disapproval to their father. Jacob cursed these boys and cut of their destinies and inheritance.

Many fathers reduce their sons to all the wrong they have done.

They never let the past go, but through prophesy hold them down and create a box that the son will never be able to be released from. Instead of all the potential that is within a son being released, the son is boxed in for all his wrong doings. Insecurity in a father can cause this behavior pattern.

Sometimes, fathers are afraid that if they release a son, they may have competition.

Of course, this is not the heart of any truly mature father, nor is it a truly wholesome pattern for fathering. This now places an unwholesome pattern into the son and keeps him locked into his past. Insecure men such as these should not function in the role of a father until this character flaw is dealt with.

In (Deuteronomy 33), one such father said to Rueben, "*You will not excel*", and to Simeon and Levi that they would be cursed for their anger. We must remember that it was not just the son who walked in this blessing or curse, but also the generations to follow.

Now a new spiritual father, a leader over the region, Moses, arrives on the scene. Moses of course knew the story of Jacob and his sons but was not affected by the sin personally. Knowing that Jacob had prophesied death and curses over his sons, Moses now breaks and revokes the curse. Let there be no death for you Reuben or for your generations to follow, death will not be your inheritance or heritage. Moses brings Reuben and Levi back into a place of pre-eminence by his words. Jacob prophesied, you will be scattered and be brought to nothing. Moses prophesies destiny and life into the son and into the generations to follow.

As fathers prophesy destiny into the lives of their sons, this helps them walk and lock into their inheritance. Fathers must never forget what God has done in their own lives, or His patience, or they will punish their sons for their mistakes. Jacob had forgotten that he was once a usurper and liar and how the heavenly Father took him and changed his character and life around for the good. If God could do it for him, why now could he not do it for his son?

The Greatest Birthright a Son Can Inherit

The greatest inheritance is peace! Blessed are the peacemakers, they are called the sons of God. The secret to walking in power is to walk in **forgiveness**. Forgive, and cut it off. Not the person, but the act. Don't talk about it, don't rehearse it in your mind, don't seek retribution or revenge or dwell on it, just cut it off. Whoever we forgive, Jesus says He forgives; whomever we hold offense against, He will not forgive either. This is apostolic doctrine, one in which we have not yet walked in, in fullness or power.

Remember, that once you have forgiven, the one you hold nothing against, no longer has the ability to control and manipulate you. This is the key to breaking free from your past. A powerful verse. This is apostolic power, one that can bring a new dimension into the life of the son and the house to which the son is connected. Blessed-empowered to prosper and have the ability to propel forward with momentum are the peacemakers, **they shall be called sons!**

The Divine Heritage Passed Down To the Sons

...you shall not bow down to them or serve them. For I, the Lord your God, am a jealous God, visiting the iniquity of the fathers on the children to the third and fourth generations of those who hate Me, but showing mercy to thousands, to those who love Me and keep My commandments (Exodus 20:5-6).

Not only are the sins visited through a lineage, but the righteousness of the fathers will also be visited down to the thousand generations.

God is concerned about our heritage. How do we break the power of the sins of the fathers? Through repentance and positioning to receive a new heritage and a new DNA, then the heritage is changed for generations to come. By Jesus, the Son of God, seeking forgiveness on our behalf, He set into motion a generation of righteousness that would come forth.

Timothy, Paul's spiritual son, led the church in righteousness after Paul died and affected many generations in the future. By connecting to Paul as his spiritual father, he was then able to cut off the heritage he received from his Greek gentile father and now receive a new DNA from Paul, which gave him an inheritance that would last for generations to come.

...The Lord has said to Me, "You are My Son, today I have begotten You. Ask of Me and I will give You the nations for Your inheritance, and the ends of the earth for Your possession" (Psalm 2:7,8).

When begotten by a father and coming into covenant, sons are given the strategy to build and to reshape the earth. Galatians 4:2 says, *"There is a time appointed by a father when a son is no longer an orphan but comes into covenant and into sonship and their inheritance is the nations."*

A father lives to release an inheritance to his son. Therefore, we can become partakers of not just the blessings, but learn to partake of our inheritance. What an awesome dimension we can then live in when we walk in our destiny. Many Christians know how to live in the facet of walking in their blessing but so few know how to partake of their inheritance. This is a profound principle that will take a Christian into a new dimension in his walk with the Lord.

(Ecclesiastes 2:18-21) *...I must leave it (my legacy) to the man who will come after me. And who knows whether he will be a wise man or a fool? For there is a man whose labor is with wisdom, knowledge, and skill; yet he must leave his heritage to a man who has not labored for it* (Ecclesiastes 2:18-21).

Who are we leaving our legacy to? Who are we transferring our inheritance and heritage to? Is it evil to leave it to a man who has not worked for it and who you have not imparted your life into? We must transfer our legacy to men who have wisdom, knowledge and skill. If they don't have these attributes then we must be as Moses with Joshua, and impart these attributes into them.

When Moses imparted the spirit of wisdom to Joshua, he gave the young man the ability to be accurate when he reached the Promised Land, and to stop the enemy.

The book of the genealogy of Jesus Christ; the Son of David, the Son of Abraham (Matthew 1:1).

The book of Matthew opens the New Testament, or Covenant, with the genealogy of Christ. Such was the importance to God, that after silence for 400 years, the first words are the lineage of a Son.

Those who inherit our heritage must be men we have chosen and begotten, and that we have birthed.

We must consider those we are investing into. These men will be our successors and so must be able to carry all we have carried ourselves and walk with the stature that we have walked in.

This is why, when Cain murdered his brother and was cast into the land of Nod he cried,

> *"My punishment is too much to bear, you have banished me from my land and **I have lost my heritage**."*

An Inheritance Handed Down From Abraham; Sons are Abraham's Seed

Our father, Abraham, cut a covenant with Melchizedek; this was the most incredible family covenant cut and is still working for us today.

Abram made covenant with Melchizedek with bread and wine and brought him all his tithes. Melchizedek then blessed Abram. The blessings, remember, were apportioned to the sons. Melchizedek blessed Abram and Abram gave him a tithe of all.

This priest was eternal, he had no beginning and no end, but the Word tells us in Hebrews that this order of priests has a heritage and an inheritance. The Levitical priesthood, when Abram met Melchizedek, was seed in Abram's loins and was to have no inheritance. To tithe was to support the priesthood. Tithing to the Levitical priesthood was a temporal legality. Abram connected with this priest; he made a relationship by cutting covenant, and then he tithed. This is a powerful concept we have not tapped into yet. Where there is no covenant relationship and input developed through connection, then we should not tithe into it. So many only see the "house" as the church to which they belong as a member. They are therefore tithing into the concept of the Levitical priesthood, and have no inheritance. If they become sons of the house and form covenant relationship with the father and family of the house, then they are tithing into an order with a heritage and inheritance.

What Was the Legacy of Melchizedek?

Adam was the first king and priest of a household. This function was passed onto his offspring and lineage. As king, Adam was to have dominion, authority, rule, and power over the kingdom as head of the household. As priest, he was to sacrifice, serve, atone, intercede and worship. Here we see the beginning of the first family priesthood. As it carries on today, the father of any family must act as the head and take on the rule of king and priest.

This is when the dispensation of the father, or we could say patriarch, began. Here in the garden, Adam knew exactly his role as head of the family. This is why God also said to Adam that a man shall leave his father and mother and be joined to a wife, and then take on the role of king and priest.

It is interesting that tithing and communion is actually a function of the king and priest. It was a function instituted in the garden to be carried on by the fathers.

At the meeting of Abram and Melchizedek a significant event took place, something we rarely hear about. A new Dispensation began, and it was that of the Son! What do we mean? The Patriarchs were all heads of their families.

It was at this meeting between Abram and Melchizedek that fathering stopped with Abram. He was now to be the father through whom the seed would come. It would be passed down through Isaac, the only begotten son of promise, and not finishing until Jesus, the Son of God was revealed.

> *So ought not this woman, being a daughter of Abraham whom satan has bound... be loosed from this bond...* (Luke 13:16).

Here is a woman hundreds of years later who is crippled, and Jesus finds her in the synagogue while He was teaching. After He healed her, the Pharisees become indignant, but Jesus calls her a daughter of Abraham. This woman had a heritage as Abraham's seed and was now walking into the heritage and inheritance given to Abraham.

> *The land that I gave to Abraham and Isaac, I give to you* (Genesis 35:12).

God spoke to Jacob, and told him that the heritage He had given to his grandfather, Abraham, had not been lost, but was now being inherited today, by him. We would be obtuse to think that the same heritage is not passed on through the generations today. God says, *"I Am the Lord, I change not."* If God does not change, then the way He builds by multi–generations is still the same today. The land He gave to Abraham and wanted his son's son, Jacob, to walk in, is still the same land He wants us to walk in today.

We have seen generals in the Body of Christ walk into dimensions of the Spirit and into the "land", but sadly this land has died with them. Instead of becoming a generational blessing, it became a tomb that they now lie in. God wants the fathers of today to build sons such as Paul did with Timothy, who can take what their fathers fought for and then hand it down to the next generation, and instead of the Body of Christ losing it again, we can take it and build from there.

Their descendants had many children and grandchildren. In fact they multiplied so quickly that they soon filled the land (Exodus 1:1-7). (Paraphrased)

Fathers Keep the Family Moving Forward Toward Purpose

Fathers must become leaders and trainers of the family, commanding what is required in order to maintain momentum as they move toward the purpose.

Love makes demands and keeps boundaries. If there is no boundary or loving demand, we can be in danger of crossing the line from a spiritual dynamic into charismatic emotionalism. Strong love, which is purpose filled and driven, makes strong demands. A demand must never be by manipulation, it must have clarity so it cannot be misread, allowing seeds from the enemy to be planted into the relationship. This demand may be in the form of verbal, emotional or physical expression, but no matter how it is given, the requirement must be clear.

He had given commandments to the apostles whom He had chosen (Acts 1:2).

We need to be pushed to fuller and greater capacity; laziness must not be tolerated, so that we learn to function effectively. If there are no set boundaries to push lovingly toward, we will never be released to function into the fullness of our inheritance.

When the Most High divided their inheritance to the nations, when He separated the sons of Adam, He set the boundaries of the peoples... (Deuteronomy 32:8).

Pushing is not driving! Pushing has an element of encouragement but driving has condemnation. Fathers must provide direction and prophetic purposes so there is no mistake in the direction their sons are going.

Through the centuries our God has been clear in His directions to His people.

Just like the heavenly Father, we must also give clear directions and confirm any new directions we expect a son to take. When we are clear in our directions and impart them quickly, the ability to harness and release resources will become available to walk in. The future must be clear and keep moving in a forward direction. If there is no communication, then there is no impartation of purpose from a father. Momentum stops and this can be a time when a son looks for a greener pasture. Remember, prophetic purpose releases hope for a fulfilled future.

Chapter Five

Families – The Order of Heaven

When traveling the world ministering, I have found the greatest tragedy inside and outside of the church is the dysfunctional family unit. I see young children hanging around on our streets till the early hours of the morning and I ask myself, "where is the family?"

Today, we are seeing governments passing laws, giving rights for homosexuals to be called "the spouse", condoning "gay" marriages, allowing a person to legally change the sex they were born with, and in some nations it is discrimination for a homosexual to be denied employment in Christian schools. We see homosexuals vagrantly declaring their sexual preference up and down city streets in the name of Mardi Gras, civil rights etc. being televised and watched by thousands, while Christianity is openly mocked.

Since the beginning of time, God made man and woman, Adam and Eve or as the old adage goes, not Adam and Steve. God created man and woman to have relationship and His first command was that they go forth and multiply. Only a man and a woman can multiply. No amount of sex changes or hormonal pills will create life from two of the same sex. Teenage pregnancies, alcohol abuse, unemployment are all problems that come down to one thing, the breakdown of the family unit. Families are eternal, *"...every family in heaven and on earth..."*

Families are the very structure of heaven and therefore important to the Lord. That's why it is one of the devil's top priorities to tear down the very family structure. Winston Churchill said, "As the family goes, so goes the nation." We can also add, so goes the church. Nehemiah 4:13-14 is set in a time when Nehemiah was attempting to rebuild the wall under great opposition and persecution. Nehemiah desperately needed to motivate his men to fight, so God had him place the **fathers** in front of their families and then said to them, "....*fight for your brethren, your sons, and your daughters, your wives and your homes.*" What a great motivator! He was in fact saying, "If you won't fight for anything else, if you won't fight for any other reason, then fight for your families"

Family is the foundation of every nation!

Time for Us to Wake Up Out of Our Sleep.

We have to ask ourselves why we are seeing the breakdown of the family unit. Never before seen in the world as it is today. The Church, the spiritual family, is to be the pattern for the world to follow. Could the church have been like the prodigal son? He had been drinking and cavorting with the world then one day came to his senses, and in his state of hangover, realized he had lost it all, his inheritance, authority, even his own rights as a son. The Word tells us that when he came to his senses, he remembered his father's house. I believe we, the church, while engaging with the world, lost our rights, for example, the right to pray in school, the right for our children to be taught Christian values etc. The Church has woken up, cleared its heads of the drunken stupor and is coming home. It is this pattern, family, which is so powerful that it sparks fear in the very heart of the enemy, and he will do all he can to stop the Body of Christ seeing this revelation.

This, the pattern of family, is the pattern that defeated satan, when the Father sent His Son to the Cross.

The first Adam, man, was created with this pattern. Perhaps it will be that when the last Adam, Christ in His fullness, which is His Body, the Church, appears, that this pattern will be the very thing that will defeat our last enemy; death, which will be swallowed up in victory. This is why the enemy is so vehement in his fight against the family, both in society and the church, his ultimate desire is to destroy it.

It is the family that has the God given authority and wisdom that is needed for today's generation, not the humanistic leadership the world has embraced this last century. Only the church, the pure family that is built on biblical principles can be the measure that society can use for restructure.

1 Corinthians 15:49 says that, the last Man shall bear the image of the heavenly **Man!** The heavenly Man is the Son of God, and as sons of the living God, we also are a part of this great family. There is a family in heaven and earth and we, the sons, are now to reveal the pattern of this family, here on earth.

The Place of Validation for a Son

A Father to the fatherless... God sets the solitary in families (Psalm 68:5,6).

We must pause here, to make the assumption that every person in the Body of Christ will walk through this process or at least desire it, is wrong. Let us not make the mistake as we have in the past, of demeaning those who do not walk this path, and for those who do, that there isn't a scale of perfection, but only light shed on the path to guide the way.

We know that before we came to Christ, we were orphans, and the heavenly Father found us and placed us in a family called the Body of Christ. The progression into the next move, the Apostolic, which we are discussing here, is to say that there are smaller families within the larger family.

For many, an unexplainable hunger begins within them. They love Jesus, they love the church, but something is missing. The desire for a relationship is deeper than they have ever experienced or heard spoken about. But does it exist? Then one day, they hear a man speak and deep within their hearts they hear a cry that is unexplainable. For many, the story ends here because not even the ministers themselves have understood this process.

The Time Appointed by the Father

We have the heavenly Father as our Father, but now a cry goes out and we hunger for God to place us, not just in a church so we can attend meetings but into a "family". God doesn't place the lonely into **a family,** which is what we have been taught, but into **families!** This is a huge difference, and now it is time to find out what it really means and how the process begins.

In Galatians 4:1-7, the Heavenly Father sent His own Son, Jesus, born of a woman under the law. The Spirit of God's Son (verse 6) was sent into our hearts and caused us to cry, *"Abba Father"*. How does this work? In verse 2 we see that sons can be under guardians and stewards until the appointed time of the father, it is transition time for a son. At the sound of the father's voice a son responds and answers. It is at an appointed time that the son hears the voice of his father and now he is moved out of slavery and into sonship. Although the time is in the heart of the spiritual father, we must remember it is the work of the Holy Spirit within the father; it can't be forced, manipulated or copied.

Beware; the enemy of Pride!

It is here that we must add a note of caution! This is an exciting time, especially for a spiritual father, he is preaching and the response given is different than ever before.

People don't just like his delivery as before, but now a work of the Spirit is happening that they have not previously experienced, a relationship is starting.

Timothy was a convert under Paul's ministry, then a disciple. Then one day the relationship changed. Paul called him *"my dearly beloved son Timothy"*. Quite a statement to make, an eternal one, a very serious one at that. In this apostolic move, I have seen excitement on both sides, ministers finding that men and women want to relate on a different level. Not just as a disciple, not just to have a mentor, but to establish a father-son relationship. Within a short period of time there comes a weariness from the depth of responsibility that this position holds, and before long the relationship is severed and it is usually the son who is left hurt and bitter. We have also seen men and women fall at a man's feet saying, "I know God has called you to be my father." Hardly a month goes by and we see the same man/woman falling at another man's feet repeating the same statement. Only one man can be your father, although many men can be fatherly toward you! Lack of knowledge causes the body to be out of order and bring reproach on the next move.

The process begins at an appointed time. The sound of the fathers' voice causes a cry to come from the heart of the son allowing the spirit of adoption to begin the process of sonship. A father's son may be in another church or even another nation!

It is here at this place of validation, by the voice of the father that moves the son from **boyhood** into **manhood** and now the son comes into his inheritance.

We read in Luke 3:22-23 that it was here at the baptism of Jesus that the voice of the heavenly Father validated His Son. Father said, *"You are My Beloved Son in whom I am well pleased."* Then straight after we see Jesus enter into His ministry and the Bible states He was about thirty years of age. It was here at the baptism that Jesus is validated by the voice of His Father and He goes from boyhood to manhood and becomes the Patterned Son. In Hebrews chapter 1, the same thing happens again after the resurrection. The Father validates His Son, saying, *"You are My Son, today I have begotten you and I will be a Father to you."* His heavenly Father repositions Jesus to be the exalted Son in the family of heaven.

> *For unto us a Child is born. Unto us a Son is given; and the government will be upon His shoulders* (Isaiah 9:6).

A boy is born, and when at baptism the Father validates Him, a mature Son was given to us. It is the mature son who carries governmental control, personally and in the city.

In Isaiah 8:18, the most amazing statement is made! *"Here am I (the prophet) and the children (sons) whom the Lord has given me. We are for signs and wonders in Israel."*

How extraordinary that spiritual fathering i.e. fathers and their sons, are there for signs and wonders to flow through. Now we see that as the early church flourished, signs and wonders were occurring daily. Why? Because it was built on fathering! Is it any wonder Paul cried out, *"Where are the fathers?"* for without this function in the church we will see fewer signs and wonders.

Divine Order in the House

We must remember this; there seems to be different types and levels of spiritual sonship. There are the sons who are connected to the father **and** the house. There are also sons of the prophet, and those just connected to the father. Neither is wrong, but when talking about the characteristics and the manner in which we may expect each son to relate, we must remember that the type of relationship in all sons can be and often will be different.

We must also address one other issue. Although we call the pastor, "the father of the house," we must never exclude the pastor's wife. The "pastor's wife", as she has sadly been identified for so many years, is also the pastor, not just the wife. Even though she may not preach or have the same obvious anointing as the pastor himself, she is still the pastor. They are both called, and are one, not just the man. In some cases it is the woman who has been called, but both are called together. Therefore, it is important that if the house is to move from members to sonship, then not only the father of the house, but his wife also must be honored as head together of the family and the house. The wife is always in submission to her husband.

Sadly in the Body today, because our revelation has not been to the fullness God would have us walk in as far as connection goes, we have unknowingly created disorder.

When a man covenants in marriage to a woman, this should not be so a man can transfer responsibility from his mother to his wife. A man leaves his mother, he doesn't marry her! Marriage completes a man's stature; he is not complete to fulfil his destiny until he has a helpmate, a woman. A woman is there to help a man fulfil his destiny of which she is a part. If a woman stays in the kitchen, she will never fulfil her role, and he will not complete his.

In Genesis, man and woman were created to rule and have dominion, as one connected being. If a man abdicates his function and does not rise into order, the woman automatically rises up and disorder reigns. Marriage completes the stature of a man. For it is together that they function, not just the man or just a strong dominant woman.

Remember, marriage is the greatest connection there is. In the charismatic move, the women left the homes to follow God, and left the men behind, and we had disorder. If the house is not in correct order, then the woman will be the one to be attacked. If the wife is working and the man isn't, we must be careful as deception can come in as the roles change.

It is here that we must be very careful as we are finding that more and more pastors today are saying, "God told me to leave my secular job and go as a full-time pastor." They only have a handful of people to support the ministry, so the wife has to return to work to support the family. This situation must be addressed, as marriage must be one road. If you choose ministry, then you must both walk the road, not just the husband, but also the wife, supporting his choice. It must be a common destiny.

Often a woman with a dynamic calling and anointing can come into the house, and because of her charisma, take on the role as mother. We must guard against this happening as the father of the house has a wife and she has this role, not another woman. Too often, a strong woman frightens a pastor and the wife feels threatened. If kept in order there should be no problem. Remember, this is not about competition, trying to compete with her anointing; it is about order in the house and fulfilling our destinies.

In the book of Judges, chapter 4, we find the story of Deborah and Barak. In verse 2, we find that because Israel had done evil in the sight of the Lord, the Lord sold them into the hand of an ungodly king. How sad to see that this nation had stooped so low as to lose their value in the sight of God. Their value was little more than if today, a man's shares on the stock market lost their value and he needed to sell them so as not to make a loss. Deborah at the time was a prophetess and a judge in Israel. She called for Barak and told him to deploy the troops for war. Deborah would not go alone to war, though she would have been able, but if she had done so, she would have created a new order for women. Although a strong woman with a strong call, she kept to divine order and submitted to a man at all times. Deborah was not insecure, she knew this was not a competition and was comfortable in her anointing and calling. Perhaps if she had given into an insecure thought or internal problems, she alone could have set a whole new order for women eternally.

A Father Will Teach a Son the succession of Authority

Fathering is not just mentoring and guidance, it's bringing sons to a place of self government where they have an understanding of authority and where they come to a place of rule in their personal lives and ministry.

To rule, one must have a clear understanding that there is a chain of authority. The Centurion soldier said to Jesus, *"I am a man under authority."* To have authority means you must first come under authority.

There will be no place of rulership unless the limits and boundaries of authority are spelt out and applied. If someone has authority, he must also be accountable to another for the authority he has. Many today in the Body of Christ are saying, "I am in charge and don't argue with me, as what I say goes". This is not authority and ruling, for there is no accountability.

To have authority, means you must take responsibility for the actions of others, as well as your own.

Authority must be used and exerted in a wholesome and pure way. Often, when a person is given a degree of authority, pride and arrogance come with it. This is why Paul said, *"Do not put a novice in an office, because a novice not only has little knowledge of the responsibility that goes with that office, but has not yet had the opportunity to rule wholesomely."* Jesus ruled with love. He had the ability not only to create boundaries, but the ability also to give authority to others, such as the seventy He sent out, without feeling insecure that his own position would be in danger.

A father's responsibility is to allow sons a realm to rule and have a sphere of authority. If not taught to rule others, then behavior patterns are not given limits in which to change and grow.

Jesus taught in depth about authority, ruling and accountability. Without being proficient in all three, there is no revelation of the kingdom. When Jesus taught about the men given talents, each man was accountable to the ruler for what he did with them, how he managed them and how he increased them. Without authority and accountability, there is no Kingdom.

When God created man and woman, they were to have dominion and bringing them to a place of self government, was to bring them to a place of understanding dominion and rule. Even though Adam and Eve were given authority over the earth and all that was on the earth, they were still accountable to God. The Heavenly Father still held Adam and Eve accountable for their behavior patterns. A son will never grow to maturity and come to a place of self-government if he is not taught correct internal patterns that will outwork into behavior patterns. If a son's behavior is wrong and there are problems that can be seen, it is not enough for a father to simply cut him off. These patterns must be changed, and the son must be given the opportunity to change and walk into a place of manhood.

The Place of Authority and Rule

If a father does not teach a son to come to a place of self-government and to rule over every enemy and wrong internal patterns, our future generations will have to deal with these same enemies.

In the book of Judges, we find that Sampson came to Gaza and saw Delilah, and it is here that he fell. Sampson means: Strong man. Gaza means: A strong place. A strong man fell in a strong place because the enemy was not totally annihilated generations before.

A giant called Goliath came from Gath and intimidated the army of the children of Israel. His purpose was to kill David from whom the seed of the King of Kings would come.

It was here that this enemy wanted to kill the worshiper whose seed would one day sit upon the throne of David. The enemy has wanted that throne ever since, and until one would come, take authority and govern, then that enemy would torment for generations.

The place where the Philistines took the Ark of the Covenant representing the presence of God, was Ashod. All of these places became the downfall of many sons, and it was not until one would rise and kill the enemy, would that enemy stop tormenting the generations that followed.

If the fathers don't take these places, they become places of defilement, discouragement, distress and defeat for their sons to follow. We only have to look at the world today and see where one president, who failed to destroy an enemy, has left a legacy to his son of not just the enemy that intimidated him, but an enemy that has grown into an organization, frightening every nation on the planet.

In the 1960's we had a generation that became a free generation of people called hippies. Soon morals slipped. In the New Millennium, a generation of rebellious, immoral sons have been raised who now have no desire for God in their lives, in fact quite the opposite.

Whose feet do we place in the box of blame? A generation that did not stand up and fight an immoral, godless enemy and that allowed God to be taken not only from the next generation, but also from the nation itself.

Just as Joshua stopped and did not take all that was given him, allowing the enemy to live and procreate in these cities, so did we. Back then, the next generation had to break through, just as today, a new fearless generation is arising. If we do not face the demons, then our sons and daughters in generations to come will have to face and fight a greater demon.

The Concept of Family Honor and Authority

In any home there is a proper chain of command, the father is the head of the house and he has the final say. It is the same in the church.

A father never has to earn respect and honor from his sons. It comes because of the stature due to his position. Stature is not something natural, it is not something we can try to promote or create. It is a place in Him we grow into according to the call on our lives. Those with true stature never have to run around with either the "small man syndrome" which will make him a bully by nature or will he have to tell everyone how tall he is, because people will see it.

Jesus, in Luke 2:52, grew in wisdom and stature. It is amazing! Remember that He was still a carpenter's son, a young boy, but there was a dynamic He carried that caused His stature to be seen by those around Him.

It is totally humanistic thinking and religious thinking to say that we earn or deserve respect because of position! Stature is a spiritual dynamic that causes men to GIVE you respect regardless of what your title says you deserve. We often see offensive behavior within Royal families, but because of their held position and title, the populace is expected to give respect, although their character and behavior do little to deserve or earn it.

Yet, in a functional family a son gives his father respect and honor due. Why? He is the father, he carries the stature that being a father produces.

The Place of Self -Government

If we look at the life of Joseph, we can see the similarities of a son who is in transition and walking through this process.

Joseph was feeding his father's sheep. Jacob, his father, loved him more than any of the others because he was the son of his old age (Genesis 37). There seems a paradox here because Jacob was around ninety-one when Joseph was born, and Benjamin was born nine years after Joseph.

What did Jacob mean? It seems that Joseph was wholly devoted to the care of his father in his old age. After the death of his wife, Rachel, Joseph became a unique helper to his father, and it seems even a mediator between him and his other sons. His father made him a coat of many colors. The coat was a mark of honor and rank and was worn, theologians tell us, by the heir of the family. We will not discuss the rights and wrongs to Jacob's obvious respect for one son over the others, but the process that Joseph had to walk before his destiny, was revealed to him.

As heir to the family, Joseph would not walk into his heritage easily; he would, as every son must, walk through a process. His brothers, full of envy, hatred and pride took Joseph, stripped him of his coat, and threw him into a pit. It is interesting that the first act of his brothers was to strip him of his coat.

His coat, remember, was a symbol of his rank, position and inheritance within the family.

It was not enough they try to kill him, but to also strip him of his inheritance and heritage. We saw in earlier chapters that the mantle a father bestows upon his son, encompasses more than the external. It includes his father's DNA, vision and heritage. Isaac, the father of Jacob, had blessed Jacob even though Jacob had received the blessing deceitfully. This shows that the blessing and heritage can be lost, or even given to another son if the father chooses. The blessing that Jacob received and now bestowed upon Joseph, was this:

> *...the dew from heaven, fatness of the earth, plenty of grain and new wine and servants; nations would bow down to him and he would be master of his brethren. His enemies*

would be cursed and he would be a blessing to those who blessed him (Genesis 27:28-29).

In Genesis 28:3-4, again Isaac blesses his son; God was to bless him, he would be fruitful, he would multiply him, make him a multitude of people, and he would walk in the blessing of Abraham.

This was still only part of the blessing he would walk in. When Joseph's brothers stripped off his coat, his brother Reuben obviously felt guilty and somewhat remorseful. Planning to return to save his brother and not allowing the shedding of blood, would eventually save his own heritage.

The boys threw Joseph into an empty cistern; it had had no water for some time and was now arid. A son will often go through an arid place in the process to his destiny.

It seems as though there is no revelation, and, at times the presence of God is far from him, for it is a place of loneliness and isolation. A son must first learn to govern his feelings when in this place. If emotions aren't governed here, he will never be able to rule in a place of influence. He must learn that his identity is not in his coat but in his relationship with God. If Joseph had allowed his feelings to govern him, he would have died in the pit before reaching the palace. He had used the coat to be his authority, the coat being a symbol of his position and rule, but now he has no coat and must learn that authority comes from within. Firstly by knowing his identity in God, and not from outside or by position or title. In each place Joseph found himself, he used his God given authority, not his title to change and dominate his circumstances. He governed them, he did not allow his circumstances to rule him.

When a son knows his identity is not in position or title, but is in the fact that he is a son, his inheritance and heritage, no matter where he is or what he is doing, makes way for him. When Joseph arrived in Potipher's house, it was evident that this slave had a blessing on his life.

Every time the seasons changed in Joseph's life, God released a greater sphere of influence for Joseph to rule and govern. In a son's life, the seasons change and a greater sphere of influence is released to him and he must learn to extend himself and grow. Joseph went from the pit to Potipher's house, to the prison and then to the palace and finally to ruling the city. This is a picture of the walk of a son.

In each place, Joseph had to rise above his past. In the pit, in Potipher's house and in the prison, he had to learn to deal with what happened yesterday and cut it off. In each place he found himself, Joseph rose above his past and circumstances and did not allow them to dictate his future.

Just as Joseph had to rise above his circumstances, we must rise above ours. Our past is only the beginning of our journey, not the **end**. Destiny is a process, our past (beginning) does not have to restrict our end. Just as Joseph did not allow his circumstances to restrict his God given vision, dream and destiny, neither must we allow our circumstances to hinder our destiny. Joseph made a decision to walk through his circumstances with his focus on tomorrow, not yesterday.

Learning to govern our thoughts, emotions and actions is the process of self–government and this is the place of ruling accurately.

To Become a Son Under Authority

We must learn how to move under subjection, breaking all rebellion and restoring the honor of functioning spiritually. A breakthrough believer will always be subject to authority. Every son must align himself to the vision and structural leadership already set in the house.

Temptation of Authority

In Luke 4:5-6, the devil took Jesus up to a high mountain to show him all the kingdoms of this world. The devil says, *"All this authority I will give to you."* Fathers must teach their sons to rule in a wholesome way and never exert their authority or position. To use a position to extract gain or leverage to a higher position is to control and manipulate. Jesus could have exposed Judas at any time in His three and a half years, but instead chose not to.

If a son is given authority, then he must know how to use that authority, to know its boundaries and sphere.

The Power of Connection

He (Timothy) will remind you of what I teach about Christ Jesus in all the churches wherever I go (I Corinthians 4:17). (Paraphrased)

Paul's ways were the ways of Christ just as a father's ways are to be the ways of Christ. This gives the son a future and a destiny, for the input he has from his father will determine his output.

Consider those who rule over you; imitate their faith (Hebrews 13:7). (Paraphrased) *For I have no one **like-minded** who will sincerely care for your state* (Philippians 2:20).

Paul said that Timothy was "like-minded," the same soul, the same thoughts, feelings and emotions. A son has the same internal configuration as his spiritual father.

This is where the shepherding movement made a grave mistake. They tapped into a new dimension but did not have the integrity or revelation to mature the knowledge they had.

A father and son must be careful as they grow into this relationship. We have either ignored this Scripture, or said that it says something entirely different. Perhaps now, we need to re-look at it and grow into the revelation of it. Paul said Timothy was **like-minded,** a huge statement; can it be backed up anywhere else?

Paul said in Philippians 2:1-2, that we were to be like-minded and to fellowship with each other. What can this statement really mean? Have we overlooked an internal dynamic that gives power to the concept of connection?

Is it possible that the soul of two people can be so knit together that they can become one? If this is possible, then it can be very close to control, and a relationship that is built on theory and not on covenant love, will always be open to manipulation and control.

*...when he finished speaking to Saul, the **soul** of Jonathan was knit to the **soul** of David, and Jonathan loved him as his own **soul*** (1 Samuel 18: 1-3).

Then Jonathan and David made a covenant, because he loved him as his own soul (verse 3).

The Word says these two were like brothers and that closeness had come through a covenant connection; they were like-minded, knit together in their souls.

A father and son will know each other's thoughts and feelings, but have a relationship that is so **pure and wholesome** that one party would never think of trying to exploit the other.

Let us look at how this connection originated so as to gain a greater understanding and insight into its internal dynamics.

...*Let us make man in Our image, according to Our likeness...* (Genesis 1:26).

God and Adam were also like-minded. They were so connected they knew each other's thoughts and feelings. Even though God created Adam in His likeness, God still allowed Adam to have his own will, mind and emotions. Although the Heavenly Father knew Adam had partaken of the tree, He could not cross the boundaries He had made at the moment of creation. An Apostolic father must always remember that apostolic fathering is not about cloning. It's about raising individual sons to fulfill their individual destinies. Even though a son's heart is to fulfil his father's vision and destiny, an Apostolic father must never abuse this in his son. How tempting for a father to be able to fulfil all that's in his heart, to do and to use his son as a slave to get there. Not only scurrilous and tempting but also very dangerous!

Apostolic fathers have the ability to restructure and redesign, as we see in Ezekiel 37. God took Ezekiel in the Spirit into the valley of dry bones. Not only was Ezekiel able to change the landscape, but also redesign the bones into a living, breathing army by the prophetic Word of the Lord. They have the ability to build by structure and design; they see a son's destiny and can build toward it by means of impartation. Not just the ability to impart the anointing, but life, spiritual genes and DNA.

Paul said in Galatians, *"I travail in birth till Christ (His Nature, DNA and Character) is formed (pushed out of you)."* Fathers reproduce into their sons, the life and DNA, which God the Heavenly Father has put within them.

Today, we have the church chasing signs and wonders, wanting these to be birthed into and then pushed out of them instead of

Christ's life. They follow signs and not a Christ-like life. You can't build on signs, because signs follow, they are not the building blocks.

Paul revealed in Ephesians, what to be like-minded was, when he talks about the mystery. He wanted us to understand the mystery of Christ, and was revealing to us how we come into the same relationship or connection that the first Adam had with God.

Let's look at this mystery in the beginning so as to gain a greater understanding of the dynamic of connection.

In the garden, Father, Son and Holy Spirit decided to create a being that was to be in the image or **likeness** of the Godhead, so as to have fellowship with Him. God's heart and desire was to increase the kingdom and kingdom heritage.

Father, Son and Holy Spirit took the dust of the earth and created this being called man, and breathed His life, and His very soul into his nostrils. Man was now a replica of the triune Godhead. He was a replica of the Father's heart here on earth. This being, called man, looked like God, talked like God, thought like God, spoke like God. When God thought, Adam knew and when Adam thought, God knew. They were so connected. They became **like–minded** and had the same **soul**. In the garden, God shows us the dynamics of connection.

God first speaks and puts a desire into Adam's soul; *"It is not good for man to be alone."* He takes the rib from Adam's side and calls her Eve.

In Hebrew, Eve means life giver. Eve was created in the image of Adam, but she had a womb so she could reproduce and carry the seed from man of the next generation. God not only wants His creation to look like Him, having the same image and soul, but to be like-minded, to carry the seed of the next generation within women, and birth it into the earth.

The enemy came into the garden, and saw something that terrified him. He saw the triune Godhead; Father, Son and Holy Ghost, three people, but connected as one. Then he sees another connection; The Godhead, and Adam and Eve, so connected, he could not tell the difference. Adam and Eve, **THOUGH NOT THE GOD-**

HEAD but connected to the Godhead, now looked like and carried the same anointing and authority and Glory as the triune Godhead.

Satan that day saw the dynamic of connection and this terrified him. Man and woman were carrying the same DNA and dynamic as God. Satan went for the soul of woman.

Why? He knew this is where the dynamic of connection begins. If he can disconnect **her** in the soul then he has succeeded in disconnecting **them** in Spirit.

Disconnection causes them to no longer live by revelation and have the glory as their covering.

Suddenly their innocence is tested and now perversion sets in. **Innocence is NOT righteousness until it is tested.** Just as Adam and Eve had the choice to listen and stay connected to God, so has every human being, from the age of innocence in the garden until today.

And the glory which You gave Me, I have given them, that they may be one just as We are one (John 17:22).

This is how Father and Son became one, like-minded. We must never forget that the dynamic of fathering flows out of an intimacy with the Heavenly Father, and a father's greatest passion is for his son to have the same intimacy with the Heavenly Father that he has. Paul said, *"I send you my son Timothy, for if you see him, then you have seen me."* Why? The answer was simple, because he was so one-with-Paul, they were like-minded.

Paul said, *"I send Timothy who is my family, when you see the family then you see me!"* Kingdom is not just making converts which we have done with moderate success, but producing sons so the heritage that was given to Abraham can be passed on. The Gospels command us to go and make disciples and the epistles by turning our disciples into sons.

Kingdom started in the garden when God said to Adam, "For this cause I give you a wife." What cause? Connection, not just friendship, but covenant relationship, where we are so joined to each other that our heritage passes on through blood. This is why God sent His Son Jesus to shed His blood, and now, "Through His Blood" we are one with the Son and can be called Sons of God. This is why the enemy wanted enmity between man and woman because they were one with each other. After the fall, it was only God who could reinstate, through the blood of animals, the heritage that belonged to man before he gave it away.

The Power of Kingdom Connection

The day Adam opened his eyes, he was no longer a lump of mud but a man with a heart and soul. He saw his Father, and that he was a connected being. The place of connection and love was the place he was driven from when he sinned and became disconnected. God's heart is that man would walk with Him in the garden, connected in oneness. Looking at Adam and Father together was a picture of true sonship. Perhaps the reason God chose David to build the kingdom was that, *"he was a man after God's own heart,"* meaning, here was a man that understood connection.

If we do not understand the principle of connection, we will not understand the principle of disconnection. Disconnecting has nothing to do with behavior. The prodigal, even though his behavior seemed that of disconnection, did not disconnect from his father. No matter what the behavior of a son, if a father is not mature to discern his spiritual state, then the relationship will become contaminated. A father, looking at behavior for signs of disconnection, will presume a disconnection has taken place and cause untold damage. Remember **connection is covenant.**

> *If you had known Me, you would have known My Father also; and from now on you know Him and have seen Him* (John 14:7).

Jesus, the patterned Son, said that if you have seen Him, then you have seen His Father because they both have the same DNA.

Spiritual fathers and sons have the same DNA. When new people come, we will automatically connect with them and bond them to the family and to the father of the house.

Paul said in Ephesians 3, that we would be partakers and fellowship with each other. What did Paul mean? Jesus said the same, *"If you know Me, then you have a connection and fellowship with the Father"*. Connecting to our Heavenly Father comes one way–at the beginning of a relationship–by words; words connect us or disconnect us. Words carry spirit and life, (John 6:63) and to unite with our Heavenly Father and the father of the house, means we must partake of their words. This is why Paul said, *"Be like minded, partake and have fellowship with each other."*

I am the bread of life... he who feeds on Me will live... (John 6:48,57).

As we partake of His words, then His life and nature is transferred into us, in the same way that Eve partook of the serpent's words and his nature and death was transferred into her.

Jesus connected all those who met Him to His Father. He came to show us His Father. Sons will connect people, not to themselves, but to the father of the house knowing, he in turn, connects them to the Heavenly Father.

Chapter Six

The Dynamic of Impartation from Father to Son

Sadly today the concept of spiritual fathering has been so badly misunderstood. We see pastors everywhere wanting to be spiritual fathers and having little or no concept of the dynamic. I hear men and women saying things like, "I have 500 sons throughout the world". My heart grieves because the very aspect of fathering is such a serious one that I often wonder who will get hurt in the end. It has often brought me to tears when I read e-mails such as, "So-and-so is my father, but I have no contact with him." Paul had few sons that we read about. Was the reason he had so few because he was capable of only truly caring for, and imparting the dimensions of the spirit effectively to these men?

Elijah had Elisha, Samuel had David, and Moses, though he had seventy leaders, had only one son, Joshua. The pattern through Scripture shows that it is only possible for someone to care for a limited number.

Raising sons must never be another notch on the belt, nor must we ever turn it into a cult where men and women follow us.

Always remember, the fruit of fathering is the relationship between brother and brother. The way we can tell what we are building is by watching the way these later relationships relate and develop, this is the acid test!

The book of 1 John is a sobering one! John says that if we say we have fellowship with Him and walk in darkness, we lie, but if we walk in the light, **we have fellowship with one another**. He, who says he is in the light and hates his brother, walks in darkness. He who loves his brother walks in light. John is talking about fathering in this chapter, and he takes the dynamic to a new level, because fathering is not just relating to a man, but also relating to each other.

The pattern for hundreds of years has not changed, we are causing men and women to follow **us**. This is evident when we see our brothers leave the church and the congregation is encouraged to cut off all relationship.

These same churches call themselves the "House of God." How can this be? It is time we took a long hard look at the word relationship and stopped making excuses for our behavior. We can border on being a cult when our people follow us in an unhealthy way and we don't allow them to form healthy relationships with others.

It is time for honesty! Jesus never lost one His Father gave Him, except Judas who fulfilled prophetic destiny, but loved and served all until the end. Today, if one disagrees with us, we hear statements like, "I am glad they're gone, we don't need them" etc. Jesus the patterned Son, never once said He didn't love them. He, at no stage said, "I have no need of Judas or Peter." With every son, whether rebellious, hard to get along with, disruptive or not, we need the revelation that **we need them**. We can choose to be a priest or a father. What is the difference? A priest will kill a sheep in the name of religion, with no emotion, but a father will die for his son.

The Dynamic of Impartation

Whoever touches you, will depend on what nature comes into your spirit. Paul said, "Lay hands on no man suddenly," because of the dynamic of divine transfer.

In any relationship, it is important to realize what you allow in and what you keep out. In the book of Samuel, we see three sons being looked after by the same father. There were the two sons of Eli, the priest, and Hannah's son, Samuel, who had been given to Eli to be raised.

Eli became Samuel's surrogate father. Eli calls Samuel his son. Scripture says that the sons of Eli were very corrupt and they did not know the Lord, but Samuel was the opposite, he knew the Lord. Even though Samuel and Eli were together, it was what Samuel allowed into, and what he kept out of his spirit that protected him.

How did Samuel know at such a tender age what was right and wrong? What protected him from the corruption that was in the temple? In 1 Samuel 2:19, Hannah, Samuel's mother, would make him a mantle (robe) and bring it to him yearly. The robes were for protection. Wearing of this robe that gave Samuel the ability to hear the voice of the Lord, and also to know his destiny. The covering of his mother during this time protected him from outside influences affecting his spirit. It was upon wearing this mantle that Samuel learnt to pray governmental prayers. He came to a place of self-government. Even though Samuel never had the Word of the Lord revealed to him, his ministering to the Lord accelerated the move of God in his life, and in Eli's. Samuel was positioned to release the Word of the Lord in a place of barrenness.

All that was happening in the natural was happening in the life of Eli the priest. As the light in the temple dimmed, Eli's eyes grew dim also.

The presence of God was no longer in the temple, and the Word of the Lord was rare in the land because Eli could no longer hear from the Lord.

Eli was a priest over nothing. The Philistines had taken the ark, but he was still performing the rituals as though it was there. In some churches today, God's presence left a long time ago, but every Sunday the same ritual is performed to an empty box. Now the ark, which was representative of the presence of God, was gone, but, as Samuel had the Word (His presence) revealed to him, the presence was no longer in the ark, but in a person. Samuel became just like the ark in his physical body. His greatest longing was for the ark; he was a priest and had nothing to officiate to but an empty box.

It is in the life of Samuel that we see the prophetic anointing rising to a new level and function than in times past. Up until the time Samuel was raised as a prophet in the temple of God, the prophetic anointing had always been released and transferred to the patriarchs through lineage and of course, on to sons. Samuel then took the anointing to a new level and function by being able to organize, consolidate and establish the nation into their prophetic destiny.

Moses was able to release a greater measure of corporate structural leadership over the nation of Israel when he laid hands on his seventy elders. When Samuel was raised up, it marked the beginning of a new era where men and women could be released into a new dimension of prophetic release and impartation.

Samuel was a prophet, priest and judge. 1 Samuel 3:20 says, from Dan to Beersheba people knew Samuel had been established as a prophet of the Lord. Samuel ministered priestly duties in the temple. He judged in the natural and spiritual realm. 1 Samuel 7:13 says the Philistines were subdued and didn't come into the territory of Israel... all the days of Samuel. Not only did Samuel have the ability to protect Israel from the enemy, but also to bring restoration to the nation when the people were restored back to serving the Lord during his days.

This is the true picture of an apostolic governmental anointing. Samuel, during his ministry, anointed two men to be king over Israel. One was Saul, who was anointed from a flask of oil. The other was David, son of Jesse, who was anointed with oil from the horn of a dead animal. Is there a difference? If so, what?

The anointing of Saul from the flask did not cost, it came from a man made source, and therefore had no life transfer. The other came through the death of an animal and cost a life to bring it. The horn speaks of the place of transfer and the horn enabled the anointing to come through a life transfer. Someone or something gave their life so that the anointing could be transferred through it. It is interesting to see that Saul was the choice of man's flesh, not God's choice, but through the cry of the people. David, on the other hand was the choice of God's Spirit. Though both men received the anointing through Samuel, only one walked in its fullness. The anointing of a king can only flow when a life has been taken. Self had to die for Christ to reign.

When the anointing comes from a man made source, it will not last, but an anointing from a source that has given its life is eternal.

When Samuel placed his mantle on those he desired, it enabled the person to operate in many dimensions. Samuel's anointing was for protection and for a covering i.e. his mantle protected Israel geographically from the Philistines. He carried a measure of the spirit that protected the nation, and David also, from Saul's murderous spirit.

When a son comes under the mantle of his father, the same thing happens and he is protected and covered from the enemy. The spirit that was on Samuel came upon both Saul and David when they were cloaked with the mantle. Soon both men were quickened by the anointing. Gifts operated in their lives as never before. They were able to see the plans of the enemy exposed and foiled, as David did when Saul tried to murder him. The leaders could see the stature that was upon them, particularly David. Samuel's anointing had a stature and a governing authority with it. David's character had to grow and be enlarged so he had the capacity to keep it and not spoil it as Saul did. To develop the dimensions of the spirit within, you must first develop the life of the vessel containing the anointing.

A Son's Birthright

Just as Samuel was born and then prepared for the day he ruled, God, today, is preparing and fashioning men all across the world for their destiny.

The destiny of a nation was in David's hands. He was born for that nation and for that day. Samuel was born to anoint David as his replacement. We must learn to keep the birthright in the spirit. It is no longer about the outside—which looks good or who preaches well but, who my son is and his ownership of the heritage and birthright.

When David killed the Philistine, the first thing Saul asked was "enquire whose son that is." Why? Only a son with a heritage and birthright could go into battle and defeat a national enemy. David, when asked about his birthright said, *"I am the son of Jesse."* David didn't go into battle for himself, but for his nation, and his father's house. Saul knew this anointing. He had once tasted it, but because he never allowed the dimensions of the Spirit to expand his character, he lost it. He was enraged with jealousy, because after tasting it and losing it to a boy, it inflamed his ego.

Saul did not understand the anointing that was upon Samuel. Saul had no understanding of the Kingdom. After being anointed, Saul went back to his uncle and was asked how he had found his lost donkeys. Saul told his uncle that he met the prophet and the prophet showed him where the donkeys were, but omitted to tell his uncle of the Kingdom. Saul had no understanding of the anointing's purpose and therefore did not fulfil it. The anointing was to change him so he could do exploits and defeat the enemy. Samuel understood the purpose of the anointing he carried, but Saul didn't. Sons must understand what their fathers carry, and the enemy they fight, for the sons will carry and fight it also.

We can see this picture clearly today as we watch world politics. In the U.S.A., President George Bush senior's mandate was to bring peace to the Middle East and to depose (one way or another) the leader of Iraq, Saddam Hussein. He did not fulfil his purpose or destiny. Years later his son is voted in as President and now has to fulfil the same destiny and purpose his father had. This time it is not just one enemy, because the enemy was given time to reproduce and now he too has sons, terrorizing the nations.

David knew the purpose of the anointing was to defeat the Philistines; Saul used it to find donkeys. Saul then used the anointing to ravage David instead of killing the thousands he was destined to kill. David used the anointing for its purpose, to keep out the enemy.

The anointing is for challenge, setting boundaries for the enemy. Often our battles are those of our fathers, and if we don't understand who our father's enemies are, then like Saul we are defeated before we begin. So many run from preacher to preacher wanting a new anointing, but the anointing is a birthright, not just a new experience.

Saul saw what was on David, and saw that he could lose the nation he never really had.

The same anointing that was on Saul's spiritual father, was now on David. This was impossible to fight, and if he tried, one that would lead to tragedy. We can't fight the grace anointing that is on each other from the same father.

We see today, because of jealousy and immaturity, sons of the same father attacking the grace anointing on each other. It can only lead to tears. We must never use the anointing to attack another. We must be careful of the words we speak.

If we do not understand the spiritual dimensions of the anointing, we will never walk in the fullness of our destined purpose. The anointing breaks open nations and the wealth of cities. As you walk in it you become a target for the enemy. He recognizes the anointing, just as Saul recognized the anointing on David.

Josephus tells us, that for the ten years he was running from Saul, David spent that time with Samuel. It was during this time that he learnt poetry and how to operate the governmental anointing nationally, and was able to come into a place of self-government. It was here that David had life impartation from Samuel. Saul wanted the anointing for selfish, natural reasons; he didn't even wait for Samuel to come in the promised seven days.

He went ahead, presuming he was able to walk in the mature Spirit dimension. David, on the other hand, spent time with Samuel, growing and maturing in the stature, that one day would be his own.

Unless our spiritual fathers have died to self, the anointing cannot be released. There must be death. Birthright is a two way street. You must be dead to your own life so you can receive another.

Gehazi could not receive his birthright because he had not died to his own agenda; the bones of his father were unable to release it. Then one day, a dead soldier was thrown onto those bones and the anointing was released and life came.

Today, there are buried bones that still hold onto the anointing, ready to release it to sons. Every place our feet tread, will be the place where the anointing is released, because it is our birthright.

This is the day when the anointing from all the great men of God, from days past, will be compounded and sons will pick up their birthright and walk in the fullness of past fathers.

The Transfer of Anointing from Father to Son.

How does the anointing transfer from one generation to the next?

Moses to Joshua, Samuel to David, Elijah to Elisha and Paul to Timothy. They are all fathers who passed down, not just the natural heritage, but a spiritual heritage to those who did not have a natural lineage.

Paul and Silas went first to Derbe and then on to Lystra. There they met Timothy, a young disciple whose mother was a

Jewish believer, but whose father was a Greek. So Paul wanted him to join them on their journey. In deference to the Jews of the area, he arranged for Timothy to be circumcised before they left, for everyone knew his father was a Greek (Acts 16:1-3). (Paraphrased)

When Paul came to Lystra he found Timothy. In Romans 16:21, Paul called him a *"kinsman, a fellow worker"*, but it was not for approximately five years that he called him his son. It is obvious Paul trained Timothy from the days in Lystra, as he called him a fellow worker, but we are not certain when Timothy picked up Paul's spirit and allowed the process of transfer to be activated.

As the lives of Elijah and Elisha unfold, we can see a pattern in the dynamic of Spiritual inheritance. While Elisha was out ploughing, Elijah passed by and cast his mantle upon him.

We must remember that Elisha was not one of the sons of the prophets. It was from the lineage of the sons of the prophets that the mantle of the prophet Elijah was expected to fall. Elijah trained all the sons; he developed each one so that they would one day, progressively walk in the same anointing that he walked in.

It was obviously possible for a person who was not a prophet, or connected to a prophet, to stay with a prophet and have the ability to flow in the prophetic anointing. Elisha was not a son of the prophet, but as he followed Elijah, the anointing transferred to him. It was possible for Elijah to give the lineage of the call and anointing to someone who had not been brought up in the lineage as the others had. Elisha, through the transfer of the anointing and call, was able to pick up the spirit. By being around a prophet long enough it seems there is a transfer of the spirit they carry.

Elijah was a pioneer. His call, anointing and dimension of the spirit was one of a pioneer to the nation. He would take on the strange gods and their idols and pave the way for God to be exalted in the nation and for the hearts of the people to be softened and turned to Him. We see a farmer's son, Elisha. The next generation came forth out of Elijah–the pioneer prophet. The call of a pioneer is a sovereign call, and the life of a pioneer, and the dimension God has placed in them can be reproduced in another.

We see a great a pioneer in Moses. He set in place such things as the priesthood and the duties that would take place in the temple before the presence of God. As Moses began these dynamics, the next generation followed on to raise up successors to carry on what he had started into the generations to come, and to expand the dynamics that he began with. Not only do pioneers transfer their spirit dynamics and call, but they are also capable of transferring the internal natures into the ones who associate with them.

1 Samuel 19:20 says, that when the messengers of Saul were sent to take David, they saw Samuel as the leader of a group of prophets prophesying. Then they themselves took on the nature of the prophets and started to prophesy. The prophetic is amazing! You can come with different natures, but hang around the prophet and soon you pick up his spirit and also reproduce.

The prophetic must be released before we can ever build. This is why the enemy has tried all to destroy the prophetic, for he knows that if we get a hold of it, then not only do we have the pattern to build but also the ability to reproduce. It is the prophetic that touches the Holy of Holies and releases the fear of God. The prophetic is like a torch, it searches out things in your life. It has with it the Spirit of revelation and so the ability to reveal even the hidden things.

This spirit dimension must be transferred into the next generation so it continues to build, and then gather momentum down the line. When a father mantles his son, all the father has and is, progressively becomes the son's.

There is a danger in this because the son can think, *"As long as my father puts his coat or prays the mantle onto me, then I can automatically walk in his anointing."*

The process of reproducing the prophetic anointing in our lives is one we grow into, it doesn't happen overnight *"...he (Elisha) left the oxen and ran after Elijah..."* (I Kings 19:20).

Why did Elisha leave the oxen, leave what we might say was "his ministry." Looking after the family oxen and ground, to pursue this man who would become his spiritual father? Elisha knew that the sons of the prophet had the spirit dynamics of the prophet, but for the mantle to be placed on his shoulders now means that he walks in the call, the process of impartation was about to take place.

...Elijah said to Elisha, "What may I do for you, before I am taken away from you?" And Elisha said, "Please let a double portion of your spirit be upon me" (Let me become your rightful successor) (2 Kings 2:9).

Elisha knew that the process of succession took place in the sons of the prophet. Though he had been a farmer's son, he knew he had followed Elijah long enough so that he could pick up his spirit. Elisha knew that the double portion would go to a successor and he was determined to pursue it.

First let me kiss my father and mother (good-bye), and then I will follow with you (1 Kings 19:20).

This is the first test of a son. Kiss your family and return. What price is he willing to pay, to pursue with passion the inheritance and mantle? Many times people follow others for the wrong reasons. Today, as we network together, we see many ministers and church members connecting and relating, not for the sake of relationship, but for what they can get from the connection. Long before Elisha was ever asked what he wanted from the relationship, he pursued Elijah—for the relationship. It is not enough to pursue a man for his connections and anointing alone, it will end in a dead end street. We must connect for divine relationship.

David could have connected with Jonathan, Saul's son, for the simple reason of finding an escape from his father. Instead, he connected because of covenant and friendship. True connection is relating first, before ever seeing what may be gained from the connection. (2 Kings 2:7-8)

The double portion only comes to those who passionately pursue the one who carries it. Many want it, take it and then leave. A son will pursue the man who carries the anointing till the end. If it is taken out of time, what could have led straight into the father's house, eating from the father's table, will instead lead to a table in the center of a pig pen, eating from the table of defeat.

God's divine order is that a double portion be handed down and then increase through the generations.

...You've have asked a hard thing. Nevertheless if you see me... (Verse10)

Elisha would now have to learn how to live with what he had asked for. A son often looks and only sees the outward, he sees the anointing and the authority and the results of both. As the working of the double portion works on a son's internal configuration, the process becomes a hard place. Elisha hadn't been there to see Elijah's internal struggle and pain, and how enormous it was. The feelings of rejection and depression, even the feelings of suicide. That is what Elijah was trying to tell the young son; it would be hard, a constant, internal battle.

"Nevertheless if you see me."

In Hebrew, the statement "if you have seen me" means "if we are seeing eye to eye, intensely focusing on each other's eyes" and "is your focus on me as I keep my focus on the Lord?" A son has to be single eyed, and have myopic vision.

Elijah and Elisha knew they were connected for life. A son will be a son and remain a son for life. He will work through all the issues that arise along the way. They will walk through all the hard places together. A son keeps his focus on the purpose and the destiny, because he and his father have connected together.

We must come to the place where we honor covenant relationships; in our marriage, church and life. God connects us together to form teams in every area of our lives. We must learn the principle of partnership where we give 100% of ourselves to the other partner.

Mutual benefit is where we give 50% and so does the other party. When a relationship is based on this alone, we will find that when the relationship comes under pressure, one or the other party will fall away.

In covenant we stay, even when there is no benefit for either party. We stand by each other during the hard times and don't run blaming the other party. In covenant there is no place for blame! The relational covenant is more important than feelings or preference; we must be quick to ask for forgiveness and to forgive.

The Scriptures say, *"A brother offended is harder to win back than a walled city."* Let us not be the wall of offense, but become the wall of grace in all our relationships. Christ came to break the wall of offense between men, and then He became the wall of love forever more. Remember, we are to take the gates of the city. What city do we try to win? What is utmost in priority? It must be our friends and family.

A gate that is offended will not accept Christ or His love.

Chapter Seven

The Cut of the Father's Knife Brings Him into Covenant.

How many Christians love church? They find a new home and tell all their friends about this awesome church they have found. They love the music, Kangaroo Hop (for those of us over forty, Hip-Hop for those below that number). We take notes and go to Bible study and of course, every group that is social.

Then one day, we come to church, dressed in our latest suit, hair very "in", sit with the "in" group, and as the pastor walks up to the platform we can sense there is a difference.

Soon we go pale as we try and shrink under the pew during the message. Pastor has just been to a conference and it is obvious God met him there, he has changed. He begins to speak on "reformation!" Before today, we thought that was a word some monk used when he wrote a long essay, and with no stamp or envelope, pinned it to a door. Why today, as he speaks about reformation, am I being challenged? Why are my relationships and lifestyle being challenged? I was happy with the Holly-wood circuit and now it seems I need to change and become Holy-wood.

As the church of today is growing in numbers, we are seeing more and more programs starting up to draw people into the church. The problem with this is, that when we get people through programs, we have to introduce new programs to keep them.

Programs do not change people, as they don't put in the dynamic to bring internal change.

Only a spiritual father can build the pattern of sonship and the pattern of the house into the sons of the house. As the dynamic of spiritual fathering is being revealed to the Body of Christ, some issues must be clarified. Not everybody can be a spiritual father, we can all be fatherly but this does not make us a father.

Spiritual fathering is an apostolic call. A spiritual father needs a stature that he carries and continues to develop with an in-built dynamic to be able to raise sons. The title of pastor does not necessarily allow a person to walk into this concept. Spiritual fathering is the same process as natural parenting. A thirteen year old may be physically capable of producing a child but he is not mature enough emotionally, or will have the wisdom to be a father and raise a child.

An uncle or elder brother, or even a leader in the church, may be fatherly to a person but is not the father. If these things are not illuminated, then we will bring confusion into the dimension of the apostolic and contaminate this new move.

Just because a leader is a children's or youth pastor, does not necessarily give him the wisdom and stature to father an adult child. Fathering is not the same as leading. A children's pastor does not have the same weight of responsibility as a father, the sleepless nights, the ability to feed and to keep the child healthy etc. A youth pastor may have a certain authority in a young person's life but until he carries the weight of their behavior, rebellion, trials and tears, he can say he is a pastor, but not a father. It takes age and wisdom to father. We could suggest also, that until a man has developed through years and by experience into the process of naturally fathering babies, youth, teens, and finally adults, he is not experienced enough to walk into this dynamic without causing pain due to his inexperience and lack of wisdom.

We see women saying that they are spiritual mothers, and this too must come back into order. This is not where we take a believer and walk with them, that is mentoring.

To be a father, a man must marry, and then through the process of covenant, naturally (and spiritually), have a child. His wife must also be mature and have the ability to walk in this dynamic, with her husband. A man must not receive "daughters" if his wife is not joined with him and also fathering/mothering the women. This is an area where we see men deceived and fall. A man must remember he is responsible for the spiritual life, and this includes behavior patterns, but the moment he proceeds to enter into a woman's life he steps beyond his God-given authority and there is trouble. A father must keep the relationship wholesome and pure at all times and never allow a son to become dependent. Fathers are from whom we receive life.

Fathering Versus Training

A father must know what kind of house he is building and therefore what kind of sons he is looking for. If you are building a military base, you don't look for ballerinas.

Fathers must never attempt to father everyone. Some will not have the stature, or substance to be your son. Not everyone needs a father, and some are in your church. They are not your sons and simply have not yet heard their father's voice; you are only a guardian to them.

Fathering takes place when the pattern of your house is placed into your sons, and you remove all that is not according to that pattern. Just as our Heavenly Father does after our salvation. He begins to place within us His pattern and remove all that the world has pressed into our character and nature.

Fathering takes serious consideration and responsibility, and cannot be taken lightly. Fathering is different from mentoring and training. Through the years, Bible Colleges have taken people and trained them be skilled in their gifts and put within them the ability to preach with an intelligent delivery, so that they fulfil their gift and function effectively.

A father on the other hand, develops his sons. Development is to nurture a person into their in-built gifting, drawing them into their full capacity and then releasing them. A son's in-built gifts and character must be developed more than his delivery or preaching style. A father must stir a son's spirit and draw out what is there, developing him internally. Relationship does not come from behind a pulpit communicating by delivery. If we do not have sharp communication skills, we will fail personally with personal relationships. We must have our character formed within and brought to maturity;

this is where we now come into the Man-Christ. Jesus was a mature man before He became a preacher; people loved Jesus for who He was not just what He said or did.

Fathers must bring their sons into wholesomeness in every aspect of their lives, family, relationships and work life in order that they manifest Christ-likeness in their character and become the vessels Christ can flow through accurately. Bible College will develop our personalities, but these are what life, environment and the world has shaped within us and caused us to become. Jesus said to his disciples, *"...I see what you have become, how the environment and life has shaped you, but follow Me and I will **make** you."*

Amos was a farmer's son and cared for cows. Amos could moo but couldn't prophesy until God got a hold of his character and developed him from being a farmer into a prophet.

Our background will be the influence of our culture and value system. Accuracy is placed into our lives to bring us into a place of wholesomeness in our character and to change our internal make-up.

A teacher will teach from a doctrinal point of view. He does not have the ability at times to find out what people know and what is needed to take them to a new level. A father will find the condition of his sons in order, to allow them to reach new levels, not allowing them to stay where they are. When Paul came to the church in Ephesus he said, *"Have you received the Holy Ghost since you believed?"* He came into the church and straight away discerned the condition of the people, he didn't come just to preach his stock message or hold another conference.

Discipline, Punishment, Chastisement and Scourging

These are all words used in the New Testament when the process of fathering is discussed. What do they mean and how are each used in the development of a spiritual son?

*My so, do not despise the **chastening** of the Lord, nor be discouraged when you are rebuked by Him; for whom the Lord loves, He **chastens**, and **scourges** every son whom He receives* (Hebrews 12:5-6).

To understand this verse, and the pattern of disciple that the Lord uses, we must first have an understanding of the words that are used in Scripture.

We must not confuse discipline with punishment. Many in the church today, due to their lack of intimacy with the Lord, believe that God is punishing them for some unknown deed. This is incorrect, God does not punish His sons, He chastises them.

I remember some time ago a friend of mine, after being diagnosed with cancer, said that God must be punishing her for some act she committed. This was a fallacy taught by religious men who had no intimacy with their Heavenly Father so as to know His character.

1) Discipline: This is when we establish a pattern of behavior that will regulate the child's life and lifestyle to enable him to come into maturity.

Fathers must first connect and turn their hearts to the son first. It is the father who is interested in the children's lives, what they eat, their teeth, or if they are ill etc. This is the job of a parent not a sibling. A parent must take care of a son's spiritual life until the son comes to a place of self-government. You can't discipline a spiritual child as you would a natural one. Some sons come to a spiritual father when they are physically mature in years, so a way to discipline must be found accordingly. As a father connects to a son, he will soon find that a son finds his own way of entrance.

In natural families, each child relates differently to the parents. There is no right or wrong way, but the parent responds according to the entrance point of the child.

Discipline enables a pattern to be placed within a child to regulate his lifestyle. For example, when a child is growing up, parents do not allow him/her to jump on the furniture. This will ensure that one day, when visiting, the parent is assured of correct behavior from their child. "Johnny, you must not jump on the furniture as it will destroy property that does not belong to you. When you sit on the couch you keep your feet off and you sit still." A pattern has now been placed into little Johnny by placing the pattern of his family within him, now his behavior is pleasing to his parents.

When a father receives a son into covenant, he must then put a right pattern of behavior into the son. It is not enough for a father to just gather sons. He must be responsible to accurately place life changing patterns that will out-work in the son's life, and assure that the son's life will be a sweet smelling aroma sent up to the Father. If the father does not deal with the son, then you have members but not sons, and this is not fathering.

A son keeps the pattern of his father's behavior, lifestyle and internal dynamics.

What if the son does not behave according to the pattern you are trying to place into him? Do you cut him off? Definitely not! This is a covenant you have entered into. Would you cut your own children off should they choose a different pattern to the one of the house? Of course not, but in today's instant theology and technology, there is little stick-ability or commitment and we are seeing hurt, angry and bitter Christians being thrown out as though they have a sell-by date.

Sometimes a pastor will be hurt by a son and instead of trying to reconcile, (which is an apostolic doctrine and ministry) they show the son the door and then call all other pastors so the son will be out of fellowship all together. This is outrageous!

Discipline brings love and security to sons because it sets boundaries for them to live by. A loving demand is a boundary.

Deuteronomy 32:8 says, *"The Father of the inheritance sets the boundaries."* Never be afraid that a strong demand will hurt the sons, it is quite the reverse, it keeps them secure. A demand must be clear, and never tinged with manipulation. When a father has brought his son into a place of covenant and there is security in the strength of love, then the demand can also be strong. Strong love, strong demands. In Acts 1:2, Jesus gave orders to the apostles He had chosen. This then allows every son to function in his full capacity and reach his destiny.

Remember, our heavenly Father disciplines us with the rod of corrective grace, and so will the father of the house.

Rebels are never corrected!

Building by programs is fast but has short longevity; building by disciplined sons is slow and is not the established method or pattern of building. This is why, when you build on this method, and you reach a certain level, you lose some again. It is easy to become discouraged at this time and revert back to the old method and the use of programs.

Will every son do everything you say? If they do, we have to ask what is the father building, certainly not sons, but robots. If a father cannot cope with the rejection of disobedience then he is not emotionally mature enough to walk in the dimension of spiritual fathering.

2) Punishment: Punishment is different from discipline. When I punish, you did wrong, so I hit the wrong. I do not put in a pattern of correct behavior, but I just hit the wrong that was done. For example Johnny climbs on the chairs and father smacks him and says, "I told you not to do that again." No pattern of good behavior has been placed into Johnny, instead he has been reduced to the wrong that was done.

3) Chastisement: To chastise means to point the finger at. We find the Lord will put His finger on certain areas of our lives that need direct attention. This is when a certain area needs to be looked at. It is definitive and detailed. The Lord does not give us a vague suggestion of what He has found wrong in our life, but points his finger directly on the problem that needs immediate attention. A spiritual father will do the same thing, he must not be vague, but give a clear direction for a corrective behavior pattern to be placed within the son.

It is imperative that a father's chastisement to a son is not subjective. He must not correct by saying "Why did you do this to me?" He has then made the incorrect behavior to be a personal affront against him. The father should step back from the situation and with clarity, explain the incorrect pattern he sees in his son.

4) Scourge: In explaining the meaning of scourging, we can use the example of everyday dressmaking. If we were to make a dress, a paper pattern is placed onto a piece of material, the dressmaker then meticulously cuts around the paper that is secured to the material. This is done in order for the material to take on the shape and design of the paper pattern. The paper is then removed after cutting has taken place and the material is now ready to be sewn together to take on the shape of the given design. The left over material may be thrown away or used to cut another pattern.

This is where spiritual fathers must be careful not to cross the line and become controlling and manipulating. A father must talk, relating and communicating with his son. If a father does not communicate, but still expects certain behavior patterns, then we must ask if the father is exploiting the son. A father must NEVER use emotional blackmail or emotional statements to manipulate a son.

Communication is a serious dynamic and it must not be contaminated. Often an insecure minister will put himself on a pedestal and expect the son to follow him and look up to him. This is a dangerous place, for he then has to keep himself there and woe to anyone who tries to knock him off. You are not building a hierarchy, keeping someone on a pedestal to be worshipped, but a family that is built on honor and love.

A Disciple, a Mentor and a Father – Three Distinct Levels of Christianity

What do people mean when they say, "I am being fathered" or "I am a spiritual father?" We have brought much confusion to the Body of Christ because of our lack of understanding.

There are three levels when disciplining a person. Let's analyze these meanings and bring clarity to the subject.

1) Discipleship: This is the first level. When a new convert comes to Christ, they need someone mature to disciple them and to establish a foundation so new patterns can be built into their lives. This is where a person now follows our teachings. Our value system and our standards, which are Christ's, are put within them until they come to the place where they are able to walk on their own and disciple new converts themselves. This is the lowest level and one we are all familiar with.

Some may walk into the next level or stay on this level, continuing to bring new Christians through by the method of being a disciple.

2) Mentoring/Teaching: This is the second level and the one that brings much misunderstanding. Mentors are confusing this dynamic with that of fathering and are bringing confusion into the Body of Christ. Mentoring is when the person follows our life; they begin to act like us, sound like us, using the same terminology. This is when the one mentoring transfers his skills and other dynamics.

This is NOT spiritual fathering and must not be confused with it. Anyone who is mature can mentor; it is the equivalent to being a guardian or a teacher and the level of responsibility is not the same as that of a father. There is no covenant entered into, just a foundation of excellent friendship and relationship. A teacher will give patterns of tradition for the pupil to follow.

3) Fathering: The third level is the deepest and the one that requires a covenant to be made by both parties. To father, means that you want to reproduce all that is in you into the son's life. The father now wants all his dreams to flow through the son and to live out his life through the son. Sadly, most are happy to mentor but do not have the dynamic to be able to reproduce what God has placed in them into the life of another. The father can shape the son's life, form new patterns and put fresh dynamics within his son. Sons soon take on the model of the father, as Timothy did with Paul. They start to think and behave differently, and act, not as they once used to, but now in the image of their father. The life of God starts to break out of them in a dynamic way. This is the reason Paul prayed, "My little children or sons, I travail in birth until Christ be formed in you." Spiritual fathering is the principle of divine impartation. It is not about imitation as one would imitate a mentor, but where impartation allows imitation of the father's ways and life to occur.

Tutor, Fathers and My Father

In Philippians 2:19 and 1 Corinthians 4.15, Paul separates the principle of mentoring, and here we see the dynamic made simpler.

Tutor: Same as a mentor as discussed above.

Fathers: Many are fatherly and can work as a father, but not everyone can walk into the apostolic call. There are many fathers in the Body of Christ. Many are fatherly to us, but we must separate and understand the work of the three functions.

My Father: This function is personal; this is where two people have entered into covenant with each other.

Paul sent a model to the churches; the model of a faithful son, who, when seen would reveal Paul as the model and would remind them of Paul's ways. To duplicate ways is much harder and can only be done through the process of impartation. A son must learn to live his life in the same way as his father; this cannot be done through teaching, homework or a pulpit, but through relationship. Jesus spent time with his disciples; He slept with them, ate with them, and related to them. It is not enough to see someone once a year and call him a son. Let's be frank and destroy some myths. If there is no relating, there is no relationship, there is no covenant and all they are to you is a friend. The father is to know the ways of Christ, just as Paul cried "that I may know Him," and those ways are to be reproduced into the son. This is how we must build our churches. No longer on meetings, but on life transfer. If there are no models for us to follow and receive impartation from, then there is no reproduction. Paul knew Jesus so intimately that he was able to transfer and pattern His life to the churches, His worship, and His prayer life. This is how we are to build; our people are to become such a part of our lives that they represent us and not just our doctrinal beliefs and teachings.

Paul wrote letters to Timothy, and in so doing, gave him the technological download to impart to his people. If we are to change the pattern of our churches, then we must teach people to respond and act differently than the way they did in the past. Old responses keep you in old patterns of lifestyle and behavior.

We must break the mould of meetings holding our churches together and build strong relationships between each other.

The Process of Impartation (laying on of hands).

We must lay hands on our people, but not for just for another blessing. This is an old model and now outdated. We must get past the charismatic blessing model and walk into the pattern of building, where we give our people a model to copy. Learn to impart when laying hands on your people, allowing the dimensions of the Spirit to transfer from you into them. This is why Paul reminded Timothy of the time the presbytery laid hands on him. They didn't just say, "Bless you my son," but knew there had been a transfer of Spirit dimensions. After the transfer of Spirit dynamics, the son will be released to apply what has been imparted to him. Impartation creates the momentum for the gift and call to be pushed out of a person's life. Fathers of the house must keep momentum going, not just in the leadership but in the people also. If momentum is not continued, then when the church goes through a transition, people will be trapped there and this is when we lose people from the church.

If a pastor wants to transform his church from the paradigm of members and meetings, then he must also turn his heart to become a father when he is ministering. If he doesn't, he will establish members, but he will never raise sons who have an inheritance, people must be gained to our family not the pulpit.

Changing Our Roles and Using the Knife.

Exodus 4:22-26. Only fathers could receive God's promise and only fathers could give the promise as an inheritance to their sons. The promise of the land of Canaan was given to Father Abraham and then to his descendants after him.

There was one condition, in Genesis 17:10, the sign of the covenant being made was circumcision of Abraham's male descendants. The covenant was to be kept in the flesh, and if not the covenant was broken.

In Exodus 3:6-15, God speaks to Moses, saying the God of Abraham, Isaac and Jacob sent him to set the children of Israel free, and this would become a memorial to all generations.

There was one problem, Moses did not circumcise his own son, and this was the sign of a covenant breaker. It was God's command to Abraham that the sons were to be circumcised as a sign of the covenant, if this did not happen then the uncircumcised son would be out off. God was now about to deliver Israel so it was essential to impose and enforce the letter of the covenant. His wife Zipporah saved the boy's life. She understood why God Himself had come and sought to kill the lad, so she cut the boys foreskin with a stone so the boy could live.

God has a call on fathers, whether it was in the Old Testament or today, to bring their sons into covenant and this means that the flesh has to be cut off and adjusted.

Moses... is dead... arise; go over this Jordan... to the land which I am giving to them–the children of Israel... divide as an inheritance the land which I swore to their fathers... (Joshua 1:1-6).

Before Moses died, he called Joshua to him and laid hands on him. It was here that he imparted into him the spirit dynamic, dimension and transfer for Joshua to now lead the people instead of Moses.

Now Joshua... was full of the spirit of wisdom, for Moses had laid his hands on him; so the children of Israel heeded him, and did as the Lord commanded Moses (Deuteronomy34:9).

Here we see Moses taking the next generation and imparting wisdom and stature into Joshua that would allow him to stand just as he had before men. Sadly, we have taken the next scripture and declared, "We are the Joshua generation," not realizing that without a Moses, our forefathers, we have no generational heritage.

The Body of Christ has taken this verse and used it to slaughter the fathers. Moses, yesterday's move, and all who were in it, is finished. Let's arise and forget our fathers and go! If it had not been for the laying on of hands and the impartation from the patriarch to the younger man, Joshua would not have had the wisdom or the stature to go. Moses was surely dead, and the time to mourn for the man was finished, there was work to be done.

Certainly, God did not mean for the man and all his input to be forgotten, or why would Moses' name be mentioned as many times as it was in the book of Joshua? Let us not bury the dimension of God with the death or the end of a statesman's ministry. Instead, let's take all he has imparted to us and carry it into the Promised Land.

Joshua was a warrior; he was not a father. Only fathers could receive the promise, as the promise was an inheritance and covenant that only fathers passed down, and sons walked into. At Moses' death, when God told Joshua to arise, it meant he had to change his role, and also the relationship he had with the people. The people had always accepted Joshua as their warrior, but now the acid test was about to happen for Joshua. Would they accept him as their father in the place of Moses and obediently allow him to walk them across the Jordan and into the land promised to their fathers?

A warrior is able to take spoils, but only a father can give sons an inheritance.

This land was promised to their fathers, but until a father paved the way for them, they would be unable to go in and claim it. Joshua had seen the land of Canaan from a warrior's point of view. He'd seen the spoils, but now he had to look and see it from a father's viewpoint, and see inheritance.

(Joshua 5:1-5). Joshua had to circumcise the Israelites, his sons, to cut their flesh and bring them into covenant before they could take the land.

Joshua reminded the people of the word Moses gave the people. The impartation and the spirit dynamics passed on from Moses to Joshua, created the momentum for Joshua to be able to do what was imparted to him to do.

When Joshua opened his mouth, he sounded like Moses, and the people responded immediately. When he finished speaking, the people responded saying, "We will do all you tell us to do," just as Paul sent Timothy to the churches and said, "He will show you my ways".

The impartation that Moses passed onto Joshua sanctioned the people to walk through the transition of the death of one leader, and the change of leadership, without any major problems. In church today, if we have not imparted the spirit transfer and have a leadership change, we can go into crisis mode and try and hold things together because the people are nervous through the transition period. If we lose structural leadership, the church will go through a traumatic time and suffer greatly. We must build correctly and plan ahead so not to cause damage within the structure of the church.

Joshua never had a problem with rebellion, although Moses did. This is why impartation is essential because as the momentum of dynamics goes down the line, it increases.

How do we impart to sons who are not always with us? Perhaps they live in another country or town as Paul and Timothy did. They were separated but still very close. It is vital to keep contact within a relationship. A relationship is not a relationship if there is no communication and contact. We must not fool ourselves into thinking that we have a covenant bond when neither party communicates. In any family, the heart's desire of a parent and son is to communicate, and if this does not happen the relationship will break down.

The place where the Israelites were circumcised was Gil-gal (Joshua 5:8-10).

Only circumcision causes the role to change from pastor to father. For without circumcision there is no covenant.

This generation had lost their fathers in the wilderness, and losing their fathers meant they lost their inheritance, promise and rest. Unless someone rose up and changed his role, this generation would never walk into the promise. To change his role meant that Joshua had to take responsibility for destiny of the people. Many pastors are willing to take responsibility for their flocks to a certain extent, but to be accountable for someone's life and destiny is a different thing altogether. Now in the role change, he comes into a place of covenant, so that no matter what happens he will be there for the son.

Most pastors today are building their ministries, their kingdom, and using their people to do it. How many will lay down their life for a son? This is the dynamic of the father/son covenant, that no longer do I live for myself, but I live for another.

It was here at Gilgal that the past, and the reproach that it carried, was cut from the people with the covenant knife.

Pastors want to discuss a person's past, take them back through time (some to the womb) and walk people through it again. Move your sons out of the past and its defeat and into their destiny by simply cutting the past off. Take people back to Calvary; establish them on what Christ has done. His work is finished. Calvary is the only past I have, not psychology. Healing only comes at the cross. Our decision to walk in the finished work of Calvary, will now determine our destiny. The past is on that cross and the destiny is raised with Him in that tomb. We must not magnify what was, our identity must be in Him alone. When we continue to allow maintenance doctrines into the church, what we are doing in reality is allowing doctrines of hell to stay within the system. If we are honest, men and women have made money by taking advantage of our naivety and lack of knowledge, and have fed us doctrines that are not based on Christ.

In Joshua 4:19, it says that the crossing took place on the tenth day of the first month, meaning that it was during the lawful mourning period. No matter what the house is going through, the momentum should never stop during that period. We must be careful because grief will cause people to stop, but if the dynamics have been imparted correctly, and the relationship is healthy, the people are able to hear our voice, see us, and are able to touch us and we can keep them in forward movement.

When they came to Gilgal, they took twelve stones from the Jordan and set them up in that place. The name Gilgal itself means to have the reproach rolled away. It was here that the Lord spoke to Joshua, telling him to take flint knives and circumcise, not just the men of the city, but **the sons' of Israel.** Not one of those men born in the wilderness had been circumcised; they were orphans, as many of the men had died at war. But not only that, they were not in covenant. At circumcision these men are no longer orphans, but are now sons, covenant sons, according to law.

After all the males had been circumcised, they rested in the camp till they were healed (Joshua 5:8). (Paraphrased)

A son will stay in the house, where healing comes. The knife cut becomes a scar of covenant and not the pain of a wound.

If a son runs from the knife, he will be running from his purpose and his destiny.

We read in 2 Kings 2:1, that Gilgal was the first place Elijah took his son Elisha. After Elisha made the statement that *"As the Lord lives and as your soul lives, I will never leave you."* Elijah's dedication to Elisha was shown in the form of covenant.

Three things often happen when a knife (spiritual) cuts a son.

1) The son will be offended because he thought that the area cut was satisfactory and didn't deserve the knife.

2) The son finds he has some pride. Usually, the knife cuts an area that is private; something the son had well and truly hidden in the closet. Suddenly the father opens the closet and reveals it. The son becomes proud, that was his area and the father had no rights to it. To hold onto the past is pride.

3) He feels wounded and hurt. How will the son react to the hurt? Often after one cut, he will never allow anyone to get close enough to cut again, nursing the scar as though it remain a wound.

Today, a spiritual father can not take a physical knife and slice into a son's flesh. A father takes the Word of God, and as he brings his son into line, he allows the same word to become covenant between them and that now ties both their destinies together as one.

In 2 Timothy 3:10, Paul says that Timothy had carefully followed Paul's doctrine, manner of life, purpose, faith, long-suffering, love and perseverance. It was through all these things that these two men became joined in purpose and destiny.

Paul's life was not an easy road to follow; it was full of persecutions and afflictions. Timothy also had Paul's stripes in his soul, in the cut of an eternal covenant.

Though he may not have the same physical pain that a father endures, the fact that he has joined with him in purpose, means that he will be joined also in persecution and will experience in his soul the same pain, and it is here we see the cut of the knife of the covenant.

The sons of Eli were the sons of Belial, the sons of the devil, who had no respect for the Lord, nor did they know the Lord (1 Samuel 2:12).

These sons did not know discipline or correction. They ate at Eli's table, slept in the temple, watched their father officiate at the altar, and still, they did not know the Lord.

This is why it is so important to the Lord that sons receive correction, discipline and the knife of circumcision to cut the flesh. If not, then His presence is dishonored.

The Knife of The Covenant Reveals the Destiny of the Son.

When Abraham took the knife to lay the first cut on his son, what happened? (Genesis 22:9-10).

As far as we are aware, Isaac lay on the altar and willingly submitted to the knife of his father. Why? For Isaac it was an act of honor and love. He realized his father, who was going to cut him, had himself been cut with the knife before him.

The circumcision itself was a sign that his father was now tied eternally to the son's purpose and destiny.

All must be circumcised. Your bodies will thus bear the mark of my everlasting covenant (Genesis 17:13). (Paraphrased)

Greater love has no father that he would take the knife to make a covenant with his son.

Often, sons feel hurt and wounded by the knife and they want to run from the house and the father. It is when a son of the house begins to feel the pain of his father's knife, that he leaves the church, hurt, bitter and angry.

And Abraham built an altar... and bound his son... and laid him upon the altar... (Genesis 22:9-18).

Isaac had a choice, would he stay or run? By staying, he was given the revelation of who he was: **He was the son of promise.**

If Isaac had run from the knife that day, he would never have seen, that through him, generations would come, all nations would be blessed and empowered to prosper.

Running from the knife means a son may never be repositioned and may never find his identity as a son of promise, no different to what happened to Isaac. Isaac was repositioned on the altar. No longer was he the younger son, but he became the son of promise and had found his identity and destiny.

The day Abraham took his son to the land of Moriah, placed him on the wood and seized the knife, he took a risk that his son would always hate him.

If a father won't enter into covenant, then he is not a true father. A true and excellent father is one who disciplines his son. As our Heavenly Father through His Word disciplines us, so to will a spiritual father through the Word of God. When correction comes, we shouldn't see it as personal rejection. This is an area where trust must grow between father and son, so that the son remains secure in the relationship.

If a father continually reduces a son to his weaknesses and wrongs, and does not affirm his positive areas, the son will become discouraged and insecure in the relationship, his hope becomes deferred and his heart becomes sick.

And have you forgotten the encouraging words God spoke to you, His sons? My sons, don't ignore it when the Lord disciplines you, and don't be discouraged when He corrects you. For the Lord disciplines those He loves, and He punishes those He accepts as a son.

As you endure His discipline, remember that God is treating you as a son. For what son goes undisciplined by his father? All legitimate sons undergo discipline, so if you don't, you are illegitimate, and not a son (Hebrews 12:5-8).

After the initial sting has left the son's tail, he mustn't run away from home, he should stay and go through the process. Both parties now have to be prepared to sit down and discuss the issues at hand.

It may seem like rebellion, but often, the truth is that he just doesn't understand, so a father must keep asking questions to be assured that he is able to perceive all the enlightenment that the father is bringing. Remember that every son is different because God made them that way. He loves each one for his uniqueness, and therefore each one will react differently.

God builds on sons and then uses them to accomplish His will in the earth today. Fathers, what an honor you are given! You are the ones that position the vessels with accuracy, in their order and in their timing. There is one important issue that must be discussed. No father of the house can walk in that role if he himself is not being fathered. First, he must have a relationship with the Heavenly Father, one of intimacy, but he must also have a close relationship with a spiritual father. It is pride to think you can be a true father if you yourself have never walked through the process of being a son. Jesus is God; Father, Son and Holy Spirit; He was Father but submitted Himself to the process of sonship.

We have three fathers; one is God our Heavenly Father, we have our natural father and we have a spiritual father. We want God and our natural father, but not our spiritual father. It is no different to some denominations having the Father and Son, but not the Holy Spirit. You have to have all three!

We had physical fathers who disciplined us, and we respected them, how much more should we submit to our spiritual father and LIVE (Hebrews 12:9). (Jewish New Testament)

Paul was not ashamed or embarrassed to call Titus and Timothy his spiritual sons and to affirm them publicly, so that all knew these two young men were in this position. Today, we find fathers ashamed to publicly call their spiritual offspring their sons. Why? Paul wasn't, he knew the power of it and the dimension it would cause these young men to walk into. Can you imagine how they felt when these men received the letter from their beloved father?

I wonder how they would feel today, knowing that their relationship paved the way for so many young men and women to now walk in the same dimension that they themselves walked in.

A Relationship Will BeTested by Fire

At a certain level, the connection between father and son is tested, and both will have the choice to cleave to (hang onto) the covenant made. The fire of testing will always be lit at some time during the relationship; but will the relationship stand the heat?

In Ruth 1:6-17, Naomi was returning from Moab with her daughters'-in-law, for the Lord had visited His people with bread.

In verse 8, Naomi says to both her daughters'-in-law, to return to their mother's house. The mother's house is representative of where there is a heritage and inheritance. Naomi though, was heading to a place where the Lord was visiting his people with bread.

Three times Naomi pressed her daughters'-in-law to return. The third time she told them to return, she asks differently, *"Turn back my daughters,"* and it was here that Naomi changed her position. No longer was she an in-law, but here she says she *will* be their mother and leave them an inheritance and heritage.

Orpah kissed Naomi and left, but Ruth clung to her and refused to leave. Ruth clung onto her inheritance and would not let go.

Now in verse 19, the two women came into Bethlehem, and it happened that the entire city was excited because of the women. Kingdom people move cities; they cause joy to be upon the city. Because she clung to Naomi, Ruth was able to sow a seed into the city because of her inheritance and heritage. Years later, on a starry night, some shepherds, Magi and a city, rejoiced with exceeding joy because the seed of connection that Ruth and Naomi sowed, was now born, the Prince of Peace, Emmanuel, in the lineage of Ruth.

Sadly, Naomi looked at the circumstances instead of inheritance and became subjective. She cried, *"Don't call me Naomi, but Mara which means bitter."* Her negative feelings and emotions caused her to make unfounded accusations against God, and in so doing, affected her belief system. Naomi said, *"I went out full, but returned empty."* Her negative statements began to affect her position and authority. By looking at her circumstances instead of her future and destiny, she saw her loss and not the seed sown that would one day give life to the giver of all life.

Ruth had the heart of a son and clung to Naomi, making a covenant with her till death. That covenant of sonship allowed Ruth to receive the inheritance of a son. Ruth married Boaz and had a son, Obed, who was the grandfather of King David. Her heritage and inheritance now was the lineage of the King of Kings, the Redeemer of the world.

We have men and women who connect with a minister quickly, commit to being a son but not realizing the implications involved. Could it be, that until now, we have few sons really connecting to a father, but have had so many joining to an idea? We find that when the heat in the relationship gets turned up and the fire is hot, one of the party suddenly believes God has spoken to them to disconnect and leave. If the relationship was truly built on the concept of spiritual fathering, God never tells either party to leave, as the concept of spiritual fathering is grounded in, and its foundation is laid on covenant.

Chapter Eight

A Son Follows a Pattern and an Order

Every church (house) is different, and the sons that belong to the different houses must reveal the pattern for the individual home and father that they are in covenant with. Of course, no son should become a clone of the house; there must be free expression, and their own way of articulating the blueprint of the house. Each house is different, and the house he is connected to, will have its own value system and culture. We need to be different, for if we become clones, we have no effect in the spirit whatsoever.

How many times do we walk into churches and find, not only the same songs as on famous CD's, but the choir dressed the same, the song leader with the same hairstyle and clothes and suddenly you think: *what are we building?* A franchise, or perhaps a package sold by brilliant Christian entertainers.

It is such a temptation to build according to the trend of today, keep it young and fresh, but pattern is not about trend. We must know how to function in the pattern of the house. Never pressure anyone into becoming a clone of the father, as ridiculous as this may sound, but sadly the truth of it has already scarred many in the church today. All must be allowed the freedom of expression to function in individual spheres of initiative, creativity and self-expression. The stereotype church creates followers who will do little to influence society or ever affect the destiny of the church.

An insecure pastor will develop this kind of structure rather than allow sons to grow into a place of self-government, as this keeps the pastor feeling needed and on a self made pedestal. These churches become insular. They build around the man on the pedestal and soon, all activities are to enhance themselves and nothing actually touches the community. They will talk about affecting the city, but in reality they choose to draw back into their own grottos where they feel safe and secure in the system that they have built. You will find, that this sort of structure does not actually reach out to other churches and the sons are kept in a state of condemnation, never reaching their full potential as the pedestal has to maintain the "man" at all times.

The Voice of a Patterned son releases Heaven on Earth

...see that you make all things according to a pattern... (Hebrews 8:5).

God has a pattern in heaven for everything He has and does here on earth. One of His patterns in heaven is the pattern that heaven itself is built on and is named after. That is the family, based on the Father and Son order.

To see how a father and son are to build, be patterned after and develop their relationship on, all we need do is copy the pattern that has already been built in heaven.

Ephesians 3:15, tells us we are named after (or to have the authority of) the family in heaven and earth using the same pattern, order, structure and authority.

I say to you, the Son can do nothing of Himself, but what He sees the Father do; for whatever He does, the Son also does in like manner (John 5:19).

The Father showed His Son all He was to do; Jesus then built after the **pattern of the spoken word of the Father.**

Ezekiel was taken into the valley of death, to dry bones in the wilderness where life was no more. He was told to speak the word that God gave him. His voice echoed through the mountains that surrounded him and the valley of death was shaken and impacted by his voice. He used his voice to create the structure of heaven here on earth. Now we can re-shape the city and nation and create an impact to produce reformation.

In Psalm 29, we see that the voice of the Lord causes the reproductive cycle of the deer to begin. So it is with any son, no matter where he is, or what state he is in, his voice, his word can cause seeds to reproduce and give life. The voice of a son releases power and dimensions of the Holy Ghost. When a son speaks, structure comes into place, and God will never destroy anything that has the structure of His Word. When God made man, He spoke, *"Let Us make man,"* and then could not destroy what His own voice had built and established.

Building By and with Eternal Design

This is how Jesus, the patterned Son, built His life here on earth... In John 17:22, Jesus said that He and the Father were one and this was the reason Jesus did and said all that His Father showed Him. We, the church, are about to enter this dimension where all we hear and see the Father do, we will do. Not copy another man's strategies or relationship with God, but where we and the Heavenly Father are one and fulfil the prayer Jesus prayed for the church before His crucifixion.

Sons must be able to perceive and embrace the insights God is releasing to this generation so we can prepare the church for tomorrow. The church must apply the heavenly blueprint so that we become the design that society is shaped by, and not the humanistic opinions that flood the world today. Society must return to the benchmark of the family being the pattern our culture is built on which has been the pattern since before the foundation of the world. It must be the church that again redefines the social order today.

> *And the children (sons) of Issachar, who understood the times, who knew what Israel should do, their chiefs were two hundred; and all their kinsmen were at their command* (1 Chronicles 12:32).

We must build according to the eternal design, with the future being our focus in accordance to the pattern of heaven and not man. If we try to build as we have been doing, only relevant to the trend of today, we have short succession, and become irrelevant in the future. God's eternal design never becomes irrelevant; it is built on the past for the future.

On Christmas Eve 1974, in Darwin, the capital of the Northern

Territory of Australia, a cyclone of monumental proportions took place; its name was Cyclone Tracy. When Darwin was built, it was designed without taking into account the external forces that could strike at any time, and the city was devastated. What would have happened if in the rebuilding of Darwin, they had not restructured for the future, but built according to how the city was built before the cyclone? No sane person would do this of course, because if another cyclone like Tracy came again, the result on Darwin would be the same.

When rebuilding Darwin after the 1974 cyclone, a great deal of structural planning was taken into account and all the residue of the city prior to the cyclone demolished, and consideration given for the future growth and development of the city.

Have we built the church the same way? Have we tried to build on the remains of past moves of God, without seeking the eternal heavenly design and structure?

David built houses for himself in the City of David; and he prepared a place for the ark of God, and pitched a tent for it (1 Chronicles 15:1).

Today, we must have fathers in the church in a position to help us build our lives and the "house" (the church) for the future. How can we build if there is no one with the wisdom and knowledge to help us construct correctly?

Then the family leaders, the fathers, gave willingly to the building (1 Chronicles 29:6). (Paraphrased)

When the fathers willingly take their place, the church is then positioned correctly. The house will be built according to the heavenly pattern and not man's. When Paul cried out to the Corinthian church, "Where are your fathers?", it was because he knew that it was only the fathers who could "build" Christ into the believers so that the destiny of each believer would come to pass.

Most sons agree with the principle of the father and son order. Sons must do more than agree or a principle will remain a principle until it is applied. The telephone is an awesome principle, I can speak to someone in Istanbul while sitting in my home in the UK, instantly by dialing a number. If I never pick up the hand piece and dial, the telephone remains a wonderful invention, someone's principle, but never affecting my life. If I don't live the principle of being a son, apply it to my life and allow it to become my daily walk, then when the fire or knife comes to test the relationship, it will never stand.

The Revelation of the Patterned Son

*...You are the Christ, the **Son** of the living God... I say to you that you are Peter and on this rock (of revelation) **I will build My church**...* (Matthew 16:16-18).

Here Jesus clearly gave the blueprint for what the Church should be built on. The Church must be built solely on whom Jesus is, not on whom men say that He is. The Church must be built on the revelation of the relationship of the Father and Son for only the Father can reveal the blueprint for building.

What was the work of the Patterned Son? He was the beloved Son from the foundation of the world. He became the obedient Son as He walked the earth for 33 years. He was the crucified Son on the cross. He rose from the dead and became the resurrected Son. He now, is the one who sits on the throne as the reigning Son; the Patterned Son of Heaven. And we are to live as He lived, obedient to the Father of Heaven, crucifying our flesh, to be sons who sit on the throne together with Him, ruling and reigning.

We were never called to be Christians, this was a name given to describe believers during the days of the early church. We are called to be sons! God never called us Christian, He never sent us a patterned Christian. God calls us sons and sent His patterned son for us to follow. We were called to produce sons who follow not our doctrinal beliefs, but our lives. Discipleship is not the ultimate, cults and religions have disciples, but only one has sons, the family of God.

The Pattern of Intimacy

...We are one... (John 17:22).

This is the purest relationship there is; intimacy of heart and soul. The heavenly pattern of the Father and Son is oneness. The Father gave the glory to the Son who then gave it to us. This is the picture of the perfect Father/Son order, where there is no jealousy, envy, competition or strife, just a relationship where the son is a recipient of the benefits the father gives.

Spiritual fathering begins with the Heavenly Father, and therefore a spiritual father must have a revelation of the fatherhood of God.

Hebrews 2:10 says, *"Father, would that many sons be brought forth unto glory."* The Father's heart is that many sons are brought into maturity and to a place of self-government. Jesus was in His Father's house learning, and growing in wisdom and stature. A spiritual father has the same desire, to bring his sons into full maturity, by finding their gifts and potential in God, and bring them to their fullness.

Rebekah saw the gifting, potential and destiny in Jacob; she trained him, nurtured him, cherished and admonished him until his full potential was reached. A father can't release all he has to his son, or nurture him successfully if he is not close to his son, in both heart and soul.

Pentecostals, Charismatics and Word Of Faith all teach wonderful foundational truths and principles, but not patterns. They rarely ever teach that Jesus was the patterned Son, or the order of that patterned Son. What then is the pattern we are to follow if this is the case? It is not enough to just know about the Word, we must know the Word, the patterned Son intimately.

Jesus was always doing His Father's business, submitting to Him and to the leaders of the day, and being taught.

My nourishment comes from doing the will of Him who sent me (My Father) (John 4:34). (Paraphrased)

At this time in Jesus' life and ministry, He could have decided to go off and do His own thing and follow His own agenda. He had the knowledge and the following. Jesus knew that His purpose, His destiny; His very life source was to do His Father's will and to finish it. The Father had prepared a pathway for the Son to walk, and the son had grown in stature, reputation and respect. How tempting for a son to now go off and follow his own agenda.

What an awesome pattern of submission, to give up all, every agenda and desire and say, "I am here to build another man's vision and dream." How many sons are willing to do this?

And if there were many, can we imagine what the church would look like?

...the Son can do nothing of Himself, but what He sees the Father do... for the Father loves the Son... (John 5:19-20).

This is the perfect pattern of heaven. The Father shows the Son all things for the Son to walk in.

Many would say I have taken Scriptures out of context and tried to build a "doctrine" around them. If Jesus was the patterned Son, then we are to walk as He walked.

The Pattern of Order

Today's generation is a fatherless generation! In the world we see children trying to divorce their parents, and rebelling against their parents' rules. They have rock stars and sport stars as role models. We have stopped disciplining our children in the guise of allowing our children self-expression, we have spoilt them, making them, as Proverbs said, a shame to mothers. Why has this been allowed to happen?

Men have not risen in the role God ordained for them as priest of their homes, and therefore we have a fatherless society. Men must rise up and take the position of leadership in the home, in the church and in society. When this begins to happen, women will feel secure in their own identity. They can trust and feel secure and protected by strong men.

Women can then function as God ordained them to, and not try and function in a position they are not capable of because of how they were created and built.

There are so many problems in churches today because there is no order. When men do not rise into leadership, this causes women to behave out of old and incorrect behavior patterns and function out of emotional insecurity. The woman's internal pattern becomes unhealthy, with rejection, jealousy and gossip causing their behavior to then be unwholesome. These old patterns will then form a habit.

...as God indeed said... (Genesis 3:2).

Why, after being told by God, did Eve disobey and partake of the fruit of the tree?

Adam had left, where was he? Was he gardening, playing golf at the opposite end of the garden, perhaps bird watching? Wherever is irrelevant, he should have been protecting Eve, which was what God had called him to do. As soon as Adam left, insecurity and doubt came in and Eve started to operate out of her five senses, and emotions.

Adam and Eve had a son, Cain whose internal problems caused him to behave in an unwholesome way. But why?

Where did Cain learn this insecurity and jealousy? It came from Eve, and it happened because Adam had not taken the role of leadership, whereby protecting Eve, not only physically from the serpent, but emotionally also. By not protecting his wife, Adam caused a cycle of death to enter their lives. Women can live with protection from harassment from the enemy, and men can live in their destiny when they rise up into the position that God ordained for them. God's divine order had been through family with the husband/father as head.

Therefore a man shall leave his father and mother and be joined to his wife (Genesis 2:24).

Although this statement is prophetic, at this point Adam's only father was God, he had no natural father to leave. Divine order is with the father as the head of the family until a son marries and becomes head of his own family. Here we see the layout and pattern God was putting into place, not only for a natural family, but for the spiritual family also.

God today still uses the same pattern and divine order for the spiritual family, *"I am the Lord, I change not."* In the "house" there is still an order and pattern, the father (the pastor) is still the head of the family. We so often find pastors going beyond the order and pattern, and trying to manipulate the flock. Nowhere in the Word did God ever manipulate.

When we look at the first pattern, the Garden of Eden, at no time did God control or manipulate Adam. God knew before the foundation of the world what Adam would do, but let him walk the hardest path of all, and then let his own Son walk the Via Dolorosa, the path of death, because of that one man's decision. God could have changed the destiny of His Son's life, but was not willing to control the life of Adam to relieve the suffering of His own Son, or Himself. We should never control even one life so that we affect the life of another, or our own.

When Jesus met the woman at the well, in John 4, she had been used and abused by the men of the city. She'd had five husbands and the man she was with now was not her husband. This woman would have been insecure, her self-esteem stolen and trodden on.

When the patterned Son spoke to her and asked her for a drink, she answered this stranger by asking Him if He were greater than *"our father Jacob."* The greatest bearing in every woman's life is her father. He is her first male love and every man from then on will be unconsciously measured by that love. The woman had had six men, none had loved her or allowed her to walk into her true identity, until she spoke to this man at the well. Suddenly He became her seventh Man–her perfect Man. One restored life will restore many, and the woman, now transformed, goes back to the city that had stolen from her and said, "Come, see a **Man**." The patterned Son showed her the true Father and restored back to her all she had lost.

The true, pure, wholesome love of a father will bring restoration and reformation.

Imitate me, just as I also imitate Christ (1 Corinthians 11:1).

This is the heart cry of sons, that they would find a father that they can imitate their life after. They long to reflect the image of one whose life reflects the image of the Son of God. They know that a father will raise them from immaturity to maturity, boyhood to manhood. A son must have a wholesome model to follow and to practice his ways in Christ. When a son follows his father's pattern, his behavior changes. Everything that we produce has a pattern that has been followed.

If we do not start constructing a wholesome model and pattern for the next generation to follow, they will follow the pattern of the enemy. Every child needs a pattern to follow so we must ensure we have a pure one in place.

We must take hold of the kingdom and train leaders, not according to good men, great teaching videos etc. but according to the pattern of the Kingdom of God. We have to raise the standard and then become the standard for the next generation to follow. He is Jehovah Nissi, the Lord our banner, our standard. When He becomes the patterned Son of our standard, then generations to come will follow the same standard.

If we want sons to imitate us, we must not major on the weaknesses but on the strengths. When a church becomes negative and the pastor continually prophesies that the people aren't ready yet, that they need to do more and more and more. It is more often than not because the pastor himself has no idea how to position his people so as they can function in their God given calls.

Many believe they are mature, they have the Bible and themselves and God, and they have no need of anybody else.

The unholy trinity! Me, Myself and I!

What a powerful dynamic, when Paul said in Philippians 2:1-2, to be like-minded and let there be fellowship of the Spirit. This now means that if the whole body would connect in this way, then the result would be remarkable. Here we see God revealing Himself as a generational God, with connection causing seeds to be planted to birth the next generation. God's eternal purpose and pattern was great. He saw beyond the garden and into the eternal future. He saw His Son, the second Adam on the cross and the spear in His side touching His rib. Just as Eve was the womb of Adam and was taken from his side, the Father sees His Son's side thrust through by a spear and, through the blood and water the Church, His Son's body, being birthed.

When the enemy sees a son he sees something greater, **The Side of the Patterned Son**, and the dynamic of his defeat.

Chapter Nine
Sons Are Faithful to Build

In the Church today, we see men and women striving to build their "ministries", not really too perturbed about tomorrow as long as their ministry is affective. We look on the Internet and see so many web pages for "my" ministry, telling all about "me", buy my books, my CD, but little talk about what is being built for the next generation, or for that matter, the Lord.

We can go to meeting after meeting, conference after conference and hear the same conversation, just different men and women saying it… "How many are in your church now?"

There is one misnomer here in this statement; it is not our church we are building, but His and His alone. The moment we take the building of His church into our hands, is the moment we will fail through pride.

Faithfulness; the Seed of Purpose

You and I are here today because a young woman named Mary had a kingdom concept and died to her agenda and dreams so that the seed of the Lord's agenda could come to pass.

One seed of faithfulness can cause a nation to rise and generations to turn. The day Mary said, *"Let it be done Lord, according to your Word"*, she changed the world and future generations for eternity. Her attitude was, "I will be what the world calls the lowest of low for woman (an unmarried, pregnant woman). I will lose my dignity and honor, give up all my dreams and visions that I had for the future, if that is what it will take, so as your Word Lord can come to pass."

Have you ever given it a thought that we don't really know who Mary was, we only ever know her as Mary, mother of Jesus, or Mary, Joseph's wife? Mary lost her identity to take on His.

Your faithfulness endures to all generations; You established the earth (by it) and it abides (continually) (Psalm 119:90).

Faithfulness continues into the next generation, carrying with it purpose and destiny. God created and built the earth by faithfulness, and today it is the same stone we use to build for the next generation.

With my mouth I will make known Your faithfulness to all generations. Your faithfulness You shall establish (permanently build and position) in the very heavens (Psalm 89:1-2). (Paraphrased)

Mary, the mother of Jesus, used her words to speak of her faithfulness. Her words, *"...Let it be done Lord according to your Word..."* are words that have transported through generations. Her faithfulness became the doorway for us to change the destinies of our nations, with the seed she carried in her womb, Jesus Christ, the Son of God.

If you have not been faithful in what is another man's; who will give you what is your own? (Luke 16:12).

This is the pathway; the doorway to more: serve another man's vision.

In 1 Samuel 16:1-13 Samuel, the prophet of God for the nation, was coming to Jesse's house to anoint one of his sons as king. Imagine the excitement!

"Are these all the sons you have?" Samuel asked. (Verse 11)

Here is a picture of the heart of a son. David: out in the field looking after his father's sheep.

The other sons have all been invited to the sacrifice with the prophet of God. The prophet had sanctified each son, but David had been left out and had not even been missed. Imagine the honor of being sanctified by the prophet and the excitement of wondering if you were to be Israel's future king. Today we think we have it made if a known prophet gives us a prophecy, we keep it in our Bible and listen to the tape till we know it off by heart, and here they think they may have the chance to be anointed king.

Let's look at the picture of sonship. The son is out pasturing "daddy's" sheep. Tired and dirty, he tenderly loves each one by name, singing a song to touch the heart of each sheep. When one is sick, this son will stay awake and nurse it till it is healthy again. Watching at dawn and dusk for predators, helping each ewe birth her lamb and protecting it from any harm.

When called to the house, what was he feeling as he smelt from a distance, the sacrifice? How did his heart suffer as he heard the sound of a celebration. Who did that donkey belong to why, wasn't it the prophet Samuel's? Of course, we can only surmise, but must still realize David was human like us, with the same feelings and emotions.

What a beautiful picture, faithful to Father even when it "seems" he has been overlooked and forgotten. He could have given in to temptation and felt discarded and unloved.

Often people move out of a church when they feel rejected and forgotten.

They forget God always knows where they are!

...Because I have refused him... the Lord looks on the heart... Samuel said, "Are these all your sons?"...Send and fetch the youngest, for we won't sit down for the sacrifice till he comes (1 Samuel 16:7,10,11).

This is all part of the repositioning process a son will go through. God knows where he has **moved the heart of the "house"** and **the heart of the son** so that the son can be positioned at the right time.

Jesse's heart, and the hearts of his sons and the "house" were moved and repositioned to receive David for his ultimate call. David was repositioned at the right time.

David had been faithful to the "previous generation's vision", his father and his father's pasture. If we do not understand the vision of the generation before us, how will we ever be able to successfully complete all God has for us to do in our generation?

(I Samuel 7:12-15). Jesse's the three eldest sons followed Saul into battle, but David went to the battle at his father's request, to take food to his brothers. He then returned from Saul and the battle to **feed his father's sheep.**

David had been anointed as the next king by Samuel. War is the time that a king goes into battle with his nation. David, the newly anointed king, is sent to the front lines to bring stores to his brothers, but then has to return to his father's fields and sheep.

Even though David had been anointed in front of his brothers as King of Israel in place of Saul, his heart was still concerned for his father's sheep. David was faithful to all that his father had placed in his hands. David, though a king, never lost the heart for the bleating of sheep. The prophet Nathan came to David one day after he had sinned, and it was through David's compassion for the sheep that he was able to obtain his confession. Even though David wore the crown, he never lost his empathy for his father's heritage, his father's sheep.

So David rose early... and left the sheep with a keeper (1 Samuel 17:20).

David was faithful to his father's heritage and Eliab, the eldest son's inheritance. He could have run off to war believing that the sheep were not part of his destiny: what would it matter if they were looked after or not? Indeed it was the opposite and David knew it. Without these sheep David would never have walked the path to the throne, and his heritage, the throne where the Son of God would one day sit.

Sons are Today's Reformers

Remember, this is all new territory as the church comes into the apostolic age. Sons today, are reshaping and remaking the culture of the church. The church was birthed in kingdom culture but has slowly slid into a pastoral anointing and culture. Although not essentially wrong, it meant we operated on a lower anointing. We are now shifting into a "governmental anointing" as God sees ready to release it over us.

What the sons are building today must be looked at with the view that they are shaping the very culture of the church of tomorrow. We must build with the view of staying relevant and useful, so the next generation will have a foundation that is proven and sound. In the past, many church leaders adopted the method of trial and error, even though Joseph said, *"I have learnt by the things I have experienced"*. This method is slow and not always successful, as we can be slain along the way in the heat of the battle.

If we are to continue in the revelation of the apostolic and grow with this new dimension of church growth, then we must change our thought patterns from the learned patterns of men to kingdom thought pattern – the blueprint of heaven.

This is reformation, and when we bring reformation into our nations, it will cause us to come back to the original pattern and structure the church was built on. It will not be a case of us going back to the reformers and bringing in a new denomination, but going back to the New Testament pattern for church formation.

Sons are Permanent Builders

Building on sons, is the only way we can build a lasting foundation for success. Sons assume leadership responsibility, knowing that what they are building today, they, and the generations to come, will partake of tomorrow.

They build with permanence and destiny in mind. For too long the church has tried to meet temporary needs immediately. If we continue with this thinking, we will have something for a short period then will have to dismantle it when it becomes irrelevant to the next generation. Just as a doctor wants not only to treat the symptom, but find and eradicate the cause.

We must take our people past just enjoying one experience after another. Otherwise, we will have a group of people who are camped at the tent of experience and have become nothing more than self-indulgent. This generation will look at the move of God and say, "What can we build and establish with it? What can this move do for the next generation?"

We must position sons to build and establish their future on the blueprint of Heaven. When not positioned to build, it is usually because the father is insecure, and insecure fathers keep sons in a permanent state of discouragement, inadequacy and feelings of constantly fighting opposition.

When the church is built totally around the pastor, then each person will only be interested in coming for another blessing. This is not building; it is socializing! We must be in a position to build, or we will just enjoy coming to a meeting place and not to a family that is building with common purpose and destiny.

If sons are being positioned to build, then they are being developed. Sons must be trained, enlarged and increased. Fathers must continually watch the condition of their sons. Often unseen problems can come between brother and brother and if not cut off, can cause decay within the house. We must not just deal with the outward symptom, but with the attitudes that caused it. The health of the family is the father's responsibility and not the elder brother's. Fathers must keep their sons clean and wholesome. Don't keep putting clean clothes onto un-bathed bodies. It is the father's job to wash his children.

Sons, Tomorrow's Leaders

We must appreciate that although we may not feel qualified to lead this generation, or the next to come, we have not walked this way before and that someone must be a pioneer, to seize the new frontiers.

Sons test their authority in the house. They will protect their father's sheep at any cost. It is here, when they are faced with their weaknesses and limitations, their own lives are confronted. Be careful not to allow negative thoughts to come and destroy their God given destiny. Deal with inadequacy and fear in a father's pasture, or temptation may come to discard all the hopes and vision God has given them to fulfil.

For David, after he had served his own generation by the will of God, fell asleep and was buried with his fathers... (Acts 13:36).

David was able to serve his generation well because he served the generation before him well, and was faithful to that generation. We are not serving our generation well if we do not connect to the previous and bring what God entrusted to them into a place of excellence now for the future.

We need to cultivate and esteem all the breakthroughs our forefathers made for us. When we breakthrough in areas now, it is for them, we now live their dreams, hopes and visions. Abraham never got to see the city with his natural eyes. He built the best he could, and through his sons, he saw his dream become a reality.

There must be an ability to multiply and reproduce all that the father has in his heart to do; this is how the Body of Christ can become city takers and nation changers.

Samuel that day, had such an affect on David's heart and life, that the first thing David wanted to fulfil, when he functioned as king, was to complete the vision and purpose in Samuel's heart. The day of impartation was the day the spirit of adoption fell onto David; Samuel then became David's spiritual father. Samuel's deepest yearning was to bring the ark of God back to Israel and saw it as being fulfilled through his son David.

Chapter Ten

What Is the Spirit of Adoption?

A son is drawn to his father and into house by the spirit of adoption, the same process that causes the father to receive the son. We have not perceived the spirit of adoption working in this fashion. We have seen Romans 8, and always related that Scripture to salvation. Perhaps we need to look deeper and allow the Holy Spirit to show us new dimensions and to find fresh revelation of this scripture.

For if you live according to the flesh, you will die. But if by the spirit you put to death the deeds of the flesh, you will live (Romans 8:13-15).

If you live according to your old nature you will certainly die. But if you live by the spirit, you put to death your old nature, you live. All who are led by God's Spirit are sons. For you didn't receive a spirit of slavery, but it is His Spirit that makes you sons and by whose power you cry "Abba" (Jewish New Testament).

In Romans, a son is and remains a son by dying to his carnal nature, and by continually putting to death his old man.

Revelation of sonship comes as we walk in the Spirit because spiritual fathering and the process of sonship are works of the Spirit. Walking in the Spirit allows us to perceive our need and God's desire for us to cry "Abba Father," not just an inward plea and deep yearning for the Fatherhood of God, but for the Fatherhood of God to be revealed to us through a spiritual father. God's deepest desire is that He be known to us as Father, and that we obtain a revelation of Him as our Father, not just God.

The Process of Adoption

And if you are Christ's, then you are Abraham's seed, and heirs according to the promise. But I say that an heir, as long as he is a child, does not differ at all from a slave, though he is master of all, but is under guardians and stewards until the time appointed by the father... And because you are sons, God has sent forth the Spirit of His Son into your hearts, crying out, "Abba Father!" (Galatians 3:29;.4:1-6).

Through lack of maturity the church has not inherited the promise that was made to our father Abraham. The church today, as sonship is being revealed to the body, is in a place of transition. If the fathers do not care for the sons correctly here, then we will lose many.

And I have declared to them Your name, and will declare it, that the love with which You loved Me may be in them, and I in them (John 17:26).

Jesus was saying, *"Father, I have revealed you to them* (as Father) *and will keep on revealing you* (as Father)."

Father wants us to have a revelation of His nature and character and Him as our heavenly Father, and He uses our spiritual fathers to do this.

*For this reason I have sent Timothy to you, who is my beloved and faithful son, and faithful in the Lord, who will bring you into **my ways, which is in Christ*** (1 Corinthians 4:17).

Often there is a yearning deep within men and women for a relationship, they don't understand the concept, they only know their heart longs for it.

The Revealing of Father through Adoption

In Luke 15:12-26, The son took hold of what was rightfully his, his inheritance. He had the right action but the wrong motive, and timing.

"How many of my father's servants have bread enough to spare, and I perish with hunger?" (Verse 17)

The son knew that there was food in his father's house. Bread represents life and a life source. The boy said that the servants within his father's house had a primary source that brought them life, and that was his father. His primary source had become that of a citizen of the country that fed him pigs swill.

I am no longer worthy of being called your son. Please take me on as a hired man. (Verse 19)

The prodigal son knew he was a son, but also knew he had acted as a hired hand and had asked his father if he could be taken back and then treated as a hired hand. He thought he had lost the spirit of sonship because of his behavior.

Why did the father receive his son back as a son? At the time Jesus told this story, the people still lived under the old covenant. The curse was still on sons. If they disobeyed the law, then they placed themselves under the curse of slavery. The same law that sent Noah's son, Ham, into slavery and Eli's sons, Hophni and Phineus to an early death, was the same law this son was under. Why was this boy not received back as a hired hand, a servant?

Jewish culture was as such, that when a man adopted a son, he then knew that the "spirit of sonship" was on the lad and the child could never lose his position as a son. The spirit of adoption made an adopted son, a son for life. Adoption is covenant; a father signs a legally binding document that makes a son for life.

Romans 8:15 says, *"You have received the spirit of adoption."*

And also Romans 8:23, *"Creation is waiting for the adoption of sons."*

What a powerful concept! A father's own son could lose his title of sonship, but an adopted son would never lose it. Noah's son touched the father, uncovered his nakedness and lost his sonship and became a servant to the servants. The prodigal was a natural son who could have lost the right of being a son. This is why he returned saying, *"I will tell my father I will come back as a servant,"* because when a son loses his rights as a son, he becomes a slave in his father's house.

The prodigal son's father was waiting for him to return. He called for the best robe–the mantle or father's covering, a ring signifying the family authority, and shoes representing the father's destiny and confirmation that the son had been liberated and was a free man with a family destiny. The robe, the ring and the shoes were all signs of covenant–now he can never lose his right as a son–he was now adopted.

"Father, I have sinned!" (Verse 21)

Only a son, who submits and humbly falls at the father's feet, can remain a son. His first word was father; he had made the decision to die to his life (as an heir) and as a son and this submission and death to his life, caused the connection between father and son to remain strong.

Only a son cries, "Father, I'm not good enough to be in your house, but I so badly want to come back anyway you see fit."

A hireling has a different heart, he stays in the pigpen of defeat and religion and wallows, where he convinces himself, that where he is, is good for him. He would rather go back to religion and bondage than confess his failure and shortfalls to his father.

The father here in this story gave the young son three things, a robe, a ring and shoes for his feet. He would not have walked in the fullness of what they represented overnight. He would grow into them as he matured.

With these three items, he was given the honor of walking into the governmental anointing that was on his father. The connection that was accomplished the moment the son said, "Father," was now the foundation for his capacity to walk in these areas.

This is how father and son succession begins, where a connection is made and the results of impartation flow. This father in Luke did not give him a book "Ten laws to being a great son." Instead he imparted his life into him. The killing of the fatted calf was the cutting of covenant between father and son and it was through this covenant the father imparted his life into his son.

The ring represented a greater authority. Not only would he function in the authority he had as a son, but in his father's authority also. A Christian who is connected to a spiritual father, has a dimension of authority that, sadly, the church has not tapped into yet.

The seven sons of Sceva, tried to cast a demon out of a person. Their father was a devout Jew, a chief priest, but religion does not have either power or authority over the enemy. A son's father must have a certain realm of authority if he is to wear his ring. The evil spirit answered them and said, *"Jesus I know, and Paul I know, but who are you?"* (Acts 19:14-15).

Here we see that Paul had authority over the demonic realm. They knew his name, and if these young men had been sons of Paul, then they too would have inherited the authority that Paul had. Today, we have the revelation that spiritual fathering provides us an ability to function in a greater dimension of authority than we would if we were independent. The prodigal had bestowed upon him his father's ring, he was now his father's son and as such walked in his father's authority.

The mantle represents the anointing. This son would no longer just function in his own anointing, but, just as Elijah threw the mantle onto his son Elisha, and Elisha was then able to walk in a double anointing, so too was the prodigal son.

What was it that made this son different from the older son? Why did the father make a covenant, a deeper relationship, connection and impartation into the life of the young son? Why did the young son get the privilege of entering into covenant with the father and receive the inheritance of the ring, the mantle and the shoes that were the rightful inheritance of the older son?

The answer is simple, **Connection.** That day, the spirit of adoption, connected both father and son. That day, the younger son was adopted as though he was the elder and all rights, and privileges fell onto him, because of the spirit of adoption.

The young son's first word was, "father," and even though his actions were deemed worthy of a life of servant-hood, his heart was that of a son. The other son broke his connection to his father.

And he called one of the hired servants and said... (Verse 26). (Paraphrased)

A hireling will speak to another member of the congregation, and usually, one who is neither part of the structural leadership to resolve any issues. He will not go to the father of the house.

The older son here in this story breaks the connection and then asks what is happening in the house.

The older brother was very angry and wouldn't go in. The father came out and begged him (Verse 28). (Paraphrased)

A father can only plead so far, and then the celebration must continue. It is up to the son if he wants to come and connect to the father, or leave the house.

Another reason why the older son was so irate was because he had not been adopted, but his father had invited him into the celebration. Sadly, his decision was to stay outside. How many sons today are invited into covenant with their spiritual father, but, because of hurt, pride, anger and independence, miss out on the covenant blessing and heritage that is theirs to walk in if they would submit to the house?

A Father Becomes a Son's Primary Source (or Provisional Relationship)

The spirit of adoption brings a son into a father's house and now the father has the opportunity to be the primary source for a son to live by.

There is something overwhelming about being a mother. When a doctor places that naked newborn baby in her arms, she are given the unbelievable opportunity to fashion that child's identity and future, and to start from scratch.

When a son walks into his father's house, we must remember one thing, he has a past. He has been conditioned by his past, both in the negative and in the positive. The past of a son has to be cut off and removed so that he can be positioned to walk into his destiny. This is what happened with Paul after his conversion. He spent three years in the wilderness, connecting to God as a son, and having his past removed so that he could walk into his new calling. This is fundamentally what it means to be redefined, realigned and repositioned.

When a son walks into his father's house, he is still attached to his past, no different to when a baby is born and is still attached by the umbilical cord to the mother. There is essentially nothing wrong with the cord, for up until birth that cord brought life to the unborn child, but if the cord is not cut off from the child then the very thing that provided life to the babe, will now be the very thing that brings death. The son's past was his blessing and source of life before he walked into his father's house, but now that same past, if he allows it to sustain him, will bring him pain and death.

We are what we eat! How many of us have heard that statement and after a Christmas feast sure feel like the turkey, let alone look like it? In the spiritual, it is the same, we will start to become what we feed on and what source we partake of.

Fathers must have fresh food for their sons on a weekly basis. It is not enough for a father to just preach an inspirational message week after week. A father must prepare solid food for his sons the same as a natural parent does. Paul says in Hebrews 5:12-14, that the church was just living on milk and because of this they remained unskilled in the word of righteousness. Those who are full age, having come to the place of the fullness of their manhood, are now partaking of solid food.

Fathers must receive truth themselves and then impart that same truth into their sons.

Many in the Body of Christ will read books and listen to tapes of their favorite speakers.

This is fine in moderation, but, the food that must be partaken of most of all, should be family food. Take away is not good for a staple diet and soon the body of a child reveals that which he is partaking of.

It is not healthy for fathers to water down the food; all food must be served as adult food. Everyone must be taught to eat from the same source. Jesus said, *"Such as I have I give unto you."* He didn't water it down or give them something superficial; He gave them food straight from heaven. The source Jesus drew from was His Father. His Father gave him the food He ate and then Jesus in turn gave it to His disciples.

Spiritual fathers must also grow and expand their internal dynamics, if not, their sons will not be brought into a new dimension and manhood.

...and how I kept nothing back that was helpful, but proclaimed it to you, and taught you publicly from house to house... (Acts 20:20).

For I received from the Lord that which I also delivered to you... (1 Corinthians 11:23).

Fathers must keep downloading the food they are receiving from the Lord. Sons must be brought to, and kept at the father's level and eat what they are eating. The reason insecure fathers do not want sons kept at the level they are at, is usually because of the fear that they may be overtaken. If a father does not acquire fresh truth and impart it immediately, their sons will never grow. The standard must always be raised. Fathers must continue to be hungry and raise the level for their sons to achieve. Many pastors just regurgitate their messages; this will never feed a family.

Even the prophets of Jezebel ate at her table and thereby acquired her nature and reproduced all that she was.

In the animal kingdom a mother lion will feed her cubs the same raw food as she eats, and train them early how to obtain their own provisions. If doesn't, their instincts are not developed and they will be in danger of being attacked. A young animal's nature and instincts are developed by the food source. Take away the food source or its ability to chase and kill and its nature and instincts will be corrupted.

Realigning and Redefining; From a Saint to a Son

When disconnection from the past comes, it will be painful. The past has conditioned him; it is usually the very thing that gave him his identity and where he draws his individuality from. Gradually he will realize that he can longer walk the way he used, as a saint, but now he must walk as a son. Revelation comes from the new positioning and the new authority. The way a son responds to his new family must not be the way he responded to his natural family.It often is, so the work of a father is to take the son through the process of change so that he now he responds to his new family in a more wholesome way.

This becomes a painful procedure to the soul of any son. He

moves through the process of repositioning of who he is, realigning where he is now, and redefining who he will become.

Fathers must continue wholesome conversations with their sons, transferring spirit to spirit. As the Scripture says, *"deep calls deep,"* and as their destinies are linked together, they must connect to the same frequency. Just as Elizabeth's baby leapt in the womb when Mary spoke and greeted her, our destinies leap within us when men and women of the same frequency speak and we pick up what is in their spirit.

Romans 8:13-15 is a simple Scripture, which says, *If we do "mortify"* (degrade, humiliate, embarrass, crush, put down, kill, put to death) *the deeds* (action, conduct and activities) *of the flesh by the Spirit, we will live. For by this you have received the Spirit of adoption whereby we cry "Abba Father."*

The reality is; a true apostolic father can take the son and redefine, realign and reposition him, but, unless the father has walked the path of a son, then he will never understand the process.

The Quickening Anointing

When the spirit of adoption draws a son to his father's house, a quickening process begins that neither the son or the father can, or should stop, as painful as this can be. We have had so many hear this new catch cry of mentoring and fathering and, sadly, I hear it talked about in such a superficial way. I know that there is no revelation on either side. One cannot be drawn by the spirit of adoption and have had their flesh seared by the Spirit of God and still use flippant terms.

The quickening anointing will bring the seed that is placed into a son by a spiritual father to early maturity and bring in an early harvest.

The quickening anointing will make the gifts that have been put into sons, work efficiently and well. The things we receive from God are blessings but what we receive through impartation from a spiritual father, is powerful because this is the legacy of inheritance from father to son.

According to 2 Timothy 1:5-7, the gift imparted by the quickening anointing positions us higher. Paul took Timothy, circumcised him, and accepted him into his lineage.

Then Paul imparts into the young man saying, *"Timothy, fight a good fight, rise above the attacks and negative circumstances by stirring up the gift, because the quickening anointing imparted to you will release the dynamic that will enable you to overcome. Timothy, our destinies are linked together. I am your primary input, so through impartation you fight and win, just as I have."*

Church members need the father of the house to impart the quickening anointing so the spirit of adoption can be released to them. This puts a life transfer into them and causes an impartation from heaven so they can fight. It will connect destinies–yours and theirs. If not connected, they will never walk into the capacity where they grow into sonship.

Most church members do not have the dynamic to fight and the pastors get frustrated, instead of taking from heaven and imparting to them in order to reposition them. If they don't have a stature, then impart the quickening anointing so they gain the stature to become a son.

A quickening anointing will release a revelation for breakthrough into a new level. If sons never receive this impartation, the church never increases in its dynamic. If we don't have an opportunity for revelation to come, then we never receive keys to enter a new level. The woman at the well saw and spoke to Jesus, and through impartation, the way opened for her to receive revelation and get the key to her destiny. She said, "Sir, I perceive!" She suddenly realized and saw, not the heart of a natural father, but what was in the heart of her Heavenly Father–worship.

Mary, in the garden, said to the gardener, *"Sir, have you seen?"* He replied, *"Mary"*, and realizing He was the Lord, her eyes were opened and she was instantly repositioned. On the road to Emmaus, the two disciples were mourning their loss and as Jesus walked with them. He opened the scriptures to them and suddenly their eyes were opened too. These men were on the wrong road; the quickening anointing turned them around and put them on the road to their destiny–Jerusalem.

Many sons are on the wrong road and need the quickening

anointing to reveal Jesus to them so as they can turn around.

The quickening anointing will cause a son to break through all limitations and those things that restrict and limit him. All of those things that limit and control us in our mind and character will be brought into a new dimension by the quickening anointing.

This gives a son a new positioning and will bring him into a new dimension of maturity in Christ. This anointing is for challenge and it will challenge every area that is in need of change and help break through into a new dynamic and dimension.

A Son Must Transition into Breakthrough

Transition is the place of passing from one place to another, one position to another and from one state to another. A son in process, must never stay in the same place but continue to keep moving. The role of a father is to help him move through the process called **TRANSITION**.

Prior to breakthrough into the next phase a son will walk in, transition must occur. We must remember the destiny of becoming a son, is not an event, it's a journey, and part of the journey will be transition.

Transition is often a place of persecution.

Saul persecuted David while he was in transition.

Elijah ran from Jezebel when in transition.

Joseph found himself in prison, yet his destiny was to be a ruler.

It is a place of unpopularity, where he will be misunderstood.

They see who he is now, not who he is becoming. The place of persecution seems to be the place where he will be put on the sidelines during the time of his repositioning and redefining. He is walking into uncharted waters. Being a church member was understood and inoffensive but when he chose to walk into covenant connection, he will walk as others have, the path of discrimination.

Transition is a place of isolation.

It's a time when a son feels displaced and isolated from all those he loves. This is the time when most walk out of the father's house or decide they don't want to be a son after all. Isolation brings the dross to the top. He must embrace this time and allow the process of transition to be fully completed, instead of allowing emotions to dictate his actions. It is here that he grows to his full potential and develops his relationship with the Lord.

It was in the place of transition that David thought he should be seeing God's will done in his life, his "prophecies" coming to pass. Instead he finds himself hidden in a cold dark cave. He is an outcast, isolated from everything that's familiar. He can be in the same physical surroundings he has always been in and suddenly feel isolated from everything that's familiar. David's destiny was a throne but he finds himself sitting on a cold hard rock in a cave.

Elijah had a great victory killing the prophets of Baal, and then finds himself hiding in a cave crying, *"I am the only one left!"* The feeling of isolation had closed around him.

Daniel in bed with some hungry lions, Joseph in a prison cell. These were all places of transition. A son may not go through a physical cave, prison or a den of lions, but can still be in that place emotionally.

He can allow the cave to be either a place of death or a place where he allows the process of new life to break through into his destiny.

Transition is a place for a son to have a God encounter.

For David, the cave of Adullam, was the place of an awesome God encounter. It was the place of total surrender to Him. It is the place where connection is to God, the heavenly Father, not His power or manifestation.

In the cave, sons are shown how to have a God encounter and a new dimension in the spirit. When Jesus said, *"Father,"* the disciples knew the Father had come.

It is here that a struggle with old mindsets can pull the son back to his old identity of membership, and not sonship.

It is in transition that we receive, a new identity. Those who don't understand the concept of spiritual fathering will not understand this new move. Saul knew David as a young shepherd boy and wanted to keep him in his old identity because he could safely control him there.

Even the disciples refused to see Paul's new identity when he found Christ.

In transition, covenant relationships are repositioned and deepened.

It is in transition that God often deepens and realigns covenant relationships. These covenant relationships are the very thing God will use to reposition and realign the son so he goes to a new level. Permitting misunderstandings to come into relationships will destroy him from connecting to the next level. A nameless thief on a cross, a nobody in a place of hell and torment, embraced a new concept, **A Man called Jesus.** He made a covenant relationship with Him and his hell became his paradise. (Who he was we don't know, but we do know he was the first to experience paradise)

It is in transition that covenant relationships are vital, as it will be these relationships that help a son move through this period of time.

...This is my beloved son, in whom I am well pleased (Matthew 3:17).

For the Word is full of living power. It is sharper than the sharpest knife, cutting our innermost thoughts and desires. It exposes us for what we really are (Hebrews 4:12). (Paraphrased)

The Father's words brought approval and blessing to Jesus. Jesus knew He was still in the place of process for the divine purpose for His life to be revealed, but the Father's words helped Him through.

...and establish you in every good word... (2 Thessalonians 2:17).

Hold fast the pattern of sound words which you have heard from me... (2 Timothy 1:13).

Words are extremely powerful! When fathers and sons come into agreement with their words, this causes sons to rise into their destiny. You can't be in agreement if you are not submitted in word and will.

When two or more agree as touching anything it shall be done.

This is one of the most powerful concepts a son can walk in.

Knowing the Word is not enough; lucifer knew the Word, (he covered the Word, and was intimate with the Word, Ezekiel 28), but knowing the Word did not put him into agreement. Why? His will was never submitted, he had an independent mindset.

"I will ascend, I will make myself." God wants us to come into agreement; He doesn't care about our opinion, religion, theology, or strategies. It is about father and son saying "Let it be done Lord according to Your will, Your plans and purposes."

When Mary, as a young teenager and a virgin, found herself pregnant, her first words to the angel were, *"let it be done according to His will, I am willing to accept all the Lord wants."* Mary rose in agreement and as she rose in agreement, the destiny of nations changed. Mary stood that day at the threshold of a visitation of God with words that had been spoken in agreement.

The word on the inside of Mary was illegal! For an unmarried woman to be pregnant was an offense, punishable by death, but the angel from heaven came with the purpose of God–you will have a baby, and still be a virgin!

God, then spoke to Joseph, and told him to marry her, to protect the seed, and make it legal. God gives us these covenant relationships to protect us, and the seed within us.

The seed was to become a son, and Joseph was to guard and protect the seed till the seed grew to maturity.

If Mary had rejected the messenger that day, she would have rejected the seed and would never have given birth to the Son. Often, we are not happy with the relationships God gives us. There is no choice, these are the relationships that will carry within them the ability for sonship to be birthed.

A father's word brings realignment and repositioning so that we walk in destiny and alignment which brings focus to function effectively.

The Heavenly Father's words at Jesus' baptism repositioned Him to function in ministry. Then at His resurrection his Father's words repositioned Him to function in His positional authority.

You are My Son, today I have become Your Father (Hebrews 1:5). (Paraphrased)

A father must be so careful of his words, as they have power and ability to cut through a son's spirit.

Oh my sons, I travail in birth till Christ is formed in you (Galatians 4:19). (Paraphrased)

When Moses laid hands on his son, Joshua, he imparted wisdom and realigning within the young man. Just as Joshua positioned the priests with the Ark (the presence of God) upon their shoulders and their feet in the water ready to cross over, so it is today. Fathers position their sons with the presence of God to partake of their inheritance.

Remember the word... Moses... commanded you... (Joshua 1:13).

After Moses had laid hands on Joshua, the impartation positioned Joshua for a new level of relationship with the heavenly Father. Up to this time God had spoken only to Moses and Joshua had only watched and heard. After the impartation from Moses, Joshua heard the word of the Lord clearly himself. This repositioned Joshua for an encounter with God, so he could make his mark and finish his call.

Moses had rebellion in the camp, Joshua did not! When a son is repositioned and realigned, and dimensions of God are imparted, the momentum to go forward increases.

It is with the help of covenant relationships that a son will not stop in the process of transition, but rather keep focused on his destiny, his future, and walk through this time directly into tomorrow. The spirit of adoption is a process; it is not a one off event. If he is not careful or does not understand the process, he can actually resist or overlook the very thing that will bring him through into his heritage, inheritance and destiny.

Chapter Eleven
Sent or Went...? What a Dilemma!

No one had ever told me that there was a difference between being released and being sent. The term often used, "she went but wasn't sent," was the epitome of me. For ten years I had been in church, and please, there is no disrespect meant in my next statements, but because of lack of understanding we did not know better. Therefore before a trip, an occasional quick prayer was said and as the song goes, "Wish me luck as you wave me goodbye." On my return, after a grueling schedule, here was this woman dragging herself through the church doors, looking as though she was in need of a miracle herself, and being asked, "Did you have a nice holiday?" One time I burst into tears, after having been in several exceptionally dangerous situations in a war torn African nation. Having suffered a high fever and thinking had I slept with elephants in my bed all night, I returned to my church (of 100 members) one Sunday to be welcomed by the door greeter, as, not only a new person, but unsaved as well.

It was now I realized, that as a minister in my own right, I was just being released from the house, but my heart longed to be **sent**. The Heavenly Father didn't **release** His Son Jesus to complete His work here on earth, He **sent** Him with all the authority and anointing of heaven backing Him. The more I looked at the Word I started to see that Jesus, did not just go to any old place to preach. He didn't get an invite from a nice city, a good church that would provide a fine offering, and then depart; He would wait to hear from His Father, and go where His Father sent Him.

Jesus traveled to each city; He sat in each home, talked with each person. He had one motive–**to connect cities and individuals to His Father.** Any itinerant ministry today would be too afraid to connect their "contacts" to another, for fear of not being asked back.

For many ministers today who are afraid to connect; the common question asked them is this, "Are you frightened that you will lose your own ministry and identity?" Was Jesus anxious he would lose His identity and His internationally renowned ministry when He did the will of His Father? No! I believe Jesus knew that He was sent, a commissioned one, an ambassador from the house and family of Heaven, and His principle purpose in going was to connect others to His Father. Then within that connection it would no longer be one Son connecting and drawing, but the principle of multiplication would take effect. Many sons would come and many would work in the kingdom for the same purpose as Jesus.

Anyone who knew me, knew I was zealous to the point of stupidity where ministry was concerned; I put Arnold Schwarzenegger to shame!

We must realize though, that it's not about going out there and "blasting the hell" out of everything in sight, it's about strategically attacking an enemy. A good armed force realizes it must work together for a common purpose. Even if those armed forces are from different nations and ethnic backgrounds, they work on a united front.

Nehemiah looked at the city and said to its inhabitants, "Let us rise and build," but it's one thing to rise, and another to build. We can't build if we don't connect one to another and network together. We need drawing on each other's strengths and reproducing to further the kingdom.

To be released is easy, get some invitations, fill your diary and go, but to be sent is different. It means we draw from one another and learn the principle of interdependence, not independence.

A son is always a son. He is always connected to his father's house whether his father has sent him, released him or whatever. A father must never separate from him.

A father must never exert control over the house but remain in relationship with all his sons, whether they remain in the house or not.

The entrance for a son into his father's house is through the father. If the relationship between father and son deteriorates, then the son no longer has an entrance into the house and he loses not just a father but a family.

If a father loses the relationship with his son, he loses the door to the next generation. A father must relate to his son for the sake of the lineage that is to come.

Elijah passed his mantle and heritage onto Elisha, but the relationship between Elisha and Gehazi deteriorated because of Gehazi's personal agenda and a heritage went to the grave.

A Father Must First Receive His Son

In My Father's house are many mansions... I go to prepare a place for you... I will come again and receive you to myself; that where I am, so you may be also... If you know Me, then you know My Father also (John 14:2-7).

A father imparts to his son, and then he is sent from the father to a region to receive others into the family. If the father loses the relationship with his son, then he will also lose a region.

Fathering is the produce of apostolic grace, where there is no grace, there will be legality and death. Fathers must operate in grace continually or may lose sons, the city and the region.

Then to be Sent

...The only begotten Son, who is in the bosom of the Father... that the world may know that You have sent me... (John 1:18, 17:23).

To be sent means to go with the authority and the anointing that is within the house. When a son is sent, he goes with the corporate anointing within the Body.

The word **"begotten"** means to "commission". To be **commissioned** is to be **sent**.

At the resurrection of Jesus, His Father made the statement that He had begotten a son. Why didn't He say this at the birth of Jesus or in the eternal beginning?

A son is not ready to be commissioned until he has the ability to **produce** and **reproduce.**

A father puts all he has, and all he is into his son. His entire DNA is imparted into his son and then he sets his son apart and commissions him or sends him.

> Then he **commissioned** Joshua, **son** of Nun, and said 'Be strong and courageous, for you shall bring the **sons of Israel** into the land which I swore to them, and I will be with you (Deuteronomy 31:23). (Paraphrased)

Once the commissioning took place, there was a divine removal of the father. God buried Moses just as God buried His own Son. then Joshua theninherited the full responsibility of leading the people of God. When Elisha was commissioned, there was a divine removal of Elijah. Elisha never saw his father again, just as Joshua never again saw his father, Moses. After Jesus gave the Great Commission to His disciples, He left and was not seen again.

Many have the ability to produce but until they mature, do not have the ability to reproduce Christ within others.

Producing is not a problem for a son. Bringing someone into the revelation of salvation is not difficult. But it is a problem when a son has to reproduce the dimensions of Christ that is within himself into others, and that only comes with maturity. If a son is to be considered being sent out by his father, then he must have the ability to create and establish dimensions of the Spirit into another. Many sons want to go, but the aim of a spiritual father is not just to release his sons but also to beget (begotten) them... **to commission and send them,** with all the authority and anointing that he, the father, and the house contain.

> The Spirit of the Lord is upon me... He has sent me... (Luke 4:18).

Jesus was sent by His Father to heal, proclaim liberty, bring the recovery of sight to the blind, and set the prisoners free. The Spirit of the Lord anointed Jesus and then He was sent. Jesus was sent with an official kingdom purpose, and with that sending came the anointing. This is the same as when a son is sent from a house. He goes with purpose and within that purpose, he is able to function in the anointing of the house.

*I was... **sent**... to the lost sheep of the house...* (Matthew 15:24).

*...I have been **sent*** (Luke 4:43).

*...As Father has **sent** me, I also send you* (John 20:21).

Jesus was fully aware He was sent from His Father's house. Jesus never said, "Father release me to preach." Jesus was sent with the authority of heaven's house, and then He was commissioned **after** the resurrection, and it was here that the authority of the nations was placed upon Him.

You are My son, today I have begotten you, ask of me... (Psalm 2:7-8).

...in Christ Jesus I have begotten you... (1 Corinthians 4:15).

A son knows that he has the authority of his father behind him. If he is treated badly, and this often happens to the "daughters", then the father will try and sort out the situation. It is sad, but something that needs to be addressed. Itinerate ministers, and particularly women, are not cared for adequately. It is shameful to think that some places don't feed the minister, put them in squalid conditions or even steal the offering.

I have preached for a sandwich, or a "Thank you, you must come again."...UNLIKELY!!!

I have never been fussy, my heart is to come and build with the pastors. Those who know me, know I spend as much time in fellowship and relationship as I do behind the pulpit, but in the early days of ministry I had no father to watch over me.

I can laugh at some situations now; the time I was placed in a bed and the sheets had not been washed for months, then to be informed the child whose bed it was had a very contagious disease. I laugh now at the memories of this itinerate going to bed with a tracksuit, socks and hat on. Yet I have had other pastors who are so concerned you would think I was their natural daughter and to them I am eternally grateful.

Why have I said this? I believe it is something that needs to be addressed in the church.

We must realize that through circumstances beyond their control, there are women in ministry whose husbands can't travel with them, or perhaps they are single. What a tragedy! When some young women we send to the mission field come home on sabbatical, we nearly kill them by making them preach to earn money for the next year, instead of treating them with the honor and respect they deserve.

If you are feeling like squirming in your seat I pray you are not offended, but challenged, and realize these women are doing what God called them to do. If they are quiet and non-offensive, don't use them, treat them as Jesus treated his women ministers–with respect. Praise God for our spiritual fathers who are now saying, "Hey wait a minute, this is my girl"

Remember this statement if the word is cutting close at this time.

Some time ago, I heard a wonderful man of God when complimented on his message say, "Thank you, what I preached is not important, but what is, is, did it change you?"

Drawing from the House

Sons know they are ambassadors of their father and of the house. Of course they know that their power base is in the Lord, and that within divine order they will also draw from the house from which they are sent.

Connecting is a son's passion, and building relationships between the houses, other ministers, the father and himself is something he longs to do. The fruit of sonship is the extension of the relationship with his apostolic father, networking and functioning together to bring the purpose of the kingdom to pass.

Jesus said, *"The Kingdom of heaven is like a dragnet cast into the sea and gathering fish of all kinds."*

Chapter Twelve

Unity of the Brethren? Is it Possible in This Millennium?

This, at some point, is the heart cry of every son. Even in natural families we see sibling rivalry.

I have one boy and two girls. Why didn't someone warn me that one day they would realize the other was there, and each one would want my attention, no matter what they would succumb to in order to get it? When they are small, a mother hears a scream from the bedroom. Her legs run at a speed she never knew they could travel, her lips are moving before her brain is in action. "What happened?" Her eyes see a sight that almost leaves terror in her stomach. Her two-year old is being held off the ground by her feet by an eight-year old tormentor, who is screaming, "You ever say that, or do that again and I will drop you on your head!"

Or could it be when your eighteen year-old daughter screams and cries because her fifteen-year old sister has done it again—stolen her clothes and make up. Perhaps I am the only mother to go through this or a similar scenario, surely not! If indeed, then what did I ever do to deserve that? No, I take heart at similar situations that other parents, sons and daughters have been through, even in the Word.

Why do I ask this question or bring this whole scenario up? At some point in the life of a house, spiritual sons will go through the pain of **sibling rivalry!**

Brothers Dwelling Together In Unity... Not Likely!

Ever since God created children, it seems sibling rivalry has existed, so how does a son overcome it? The first place we see a dispute between brothers is in Genesis... the first family created.

*So He **drove** out the man; and He placed cherubim at the east of the Garden of Eden, and a flaming sword which turned every way, to **keep** the way to the tree of life* (Genesis 3:24).

The word **drove** in the Hebrew is a word that means to expel; to physically drive away from a possession. Could it be that Adam and Eve were so loathed to leave the garden that they had to be driven out? Until Christ came to redeem man, a cherubim with a flaming sword has had **to keep** the garden.

When the time came she gave birth to Cain... Later she gave birth to Abel (Genesis 4:1-2). (Paraphrased)

Cain was the first brother born and his name in Hebrew means "to acquire by my hand."

Abel was the second brother, his name in Hebrew means "breath of God." Abel was a shepherd, and when a son tends sheep, he holds a special place in the heart of God. The second son born, and then killed at the hand of a religious brother who was a shepherd. The Son who gave his life at the hands of religious men was also a shepherd.

Cain and Abel are a perfect example of sibling rivalry. Cain was jealous of Abel's offering. One of the reasons for Cain's anger was because Abel gave a tithe to the Lord; he gave the first and the best. Cain's jealousy and anger caused him to rise up and kill his brother. He compared his offering to that of his brother. This leads to jealousy, which in turn leads to anger, hatred and, taken to its limits... murder. This is an aspect where only a father can bring peace.

When Adam, Cain's father sinned, God had to minister atonement for Adam. This is why He used the skin of an animal to cover man's nakedness, and allowed man to be in the presence of God and live, because blood was shed. A priest received from the sacrifice only the skin of an animal, so here we see Adam now operating in the function of a priest, back before he left the garden. He was now to teach his offspring the truth about atonement, the coming Savior who would one day come through the seed of a woman. It would take the death of an animal to purchase back mankind, hence at Calvary. Wheat was not hung on a tree but a spotless lamb; the Lamb of God shed His blood for mankind.

Cain was accountable for his act. His father, Adam, shared with both sons the story of the garden, and both sons were to officiate as priests; one did, the other refused. This is why God was so wroth at Cain's offering. Cain knew the only way to stay in the presence of God was for blood to be shed through a priestly function.

God knew that for Cain to stay in His presence, he would need an offering of blood, not one from the cursed ground, hence the reason for God asking why Cain was angry. God knew Cain was aware of his actions.

"You will be accepted if you respond in the right way."

Every son has the power to act correctly. We all live and die by our own choices. Cain knew in his heart what to do but refused to do it, he attacked the breath of God–his brother Abel.

The way religion works and functions is to compare itself to another. It is the reason for almost every instance of sibling rivalry in spiritual sons. Each son must be confident in who they are in Christ and what their function is in Him, if not, comparisons and jealousy come between relationships. When a son walks in the flesh, he will ultimately attack the breath of God.

Sons have a special relationship. They are in covenant, and this means that they are joined together no matter what. A brother sticks with his brother even through adversity.

Murder, (and murder can even be spiritual. Jesus says if we commit adultery, murder with our thoughts then we have accomplished it), is when one not only sins against God and the one he kills, **but also against the murdered one's heritage for eternal generations.**

Sibling rivalry is a serious act. It starts with jealousy and comparisons, and when taken to the limits, a son will even start speaking death over his spiritual family. It affects not only the two sons in contention with each other, but also their heritage.

154

Joseph and his brothers were no different, except in age, but his brothers were jealous, because of two things. First, he had the coat—remember it represented the family heritage and inheritance–and second, the gift that God had given him.

Joseph obviously had an intimate relationship with his father. Many criticize Jacob for this, saying he favored the young son above the others. Instead of each of Joseph sons deciding to find a more intimate relationship with their father, they chose to eliminate Joseph, **casting blame instead of change!**

We often blame others for our distant relationship and lack of intimacy with our spiritual father or family. As soon as blame is cast, then the one casting the blame will try and eliminate the one they see as a stumbling block.

In a house, it can start by gossip and rumors till the one who is the center of the blame leaves, offended.

This seeking of attention, and the approval of a parent, or spiritual father, is the root of sibling rivalry today. In the story of the prodigal son, we see the relationship between both sons and their father. The way in which the father responded to both differently, for no other reason than their different behavior, and the way in which each son found entrance into the father's heart.

One had a formal relationship with his father, the other an intimate relationship. We must remember both boys were sons. When the younger one returned he hugged his father but the elder one stayed in the field at a distance.

Restitution of Relationships in a Family

One wonderful example of forgiveness and potential sibling rivalry is in the book of Philemon. Philemon was a prominent member of the church at Collosse. He had a slave called Onesimus who had wronged Philemon by foolishly stealing from him and running away to Rome. By divine opportunity he met Paul who then led him to Christ. Onesimus became a devoted helper of Paul.

In the book of Philemon, we see some great truths. Paul tells Onesimus to leave him, oh the ache in that young man's heart when he had to leave his father in Rome. Paul knew that there was a more important matter at hand. Philemon and Onesimus needed to resolve some issues. A time for forgiveness was needed for restoration to come.

The burden of forgiveness was not merely on Philemon, Onesimus had to return to Philemon and even risk death, in order to seek forgiveness.

Paul, this young man's father, knew he was sending his son into a dangerous situation as Philemon had every right to seek the death penalty for this young man, but Paul knew this situation between the men had to be mended for the sake of the church and the work of the ministry. Onesimus could have taken Paul's letter and simply thrown it away.

No one would ever have known, as he had escaped to another Roman City and into oblivion. He didn't! This young son showed honor to his father and to his brother and restored the relationship, and today, we have this beautiful letter of forgiveness, and reconciliation. It is so important in relationships, that reconciliation and restoration is sought.

Paul knew what could have happened but had confidence in his son and fellow brother in the Lord. The heart of a father is in this book. Christ had forgiven Paul, a zealous murderer and Paul now forgives Onesimus's foolish behavior. What is more, Paul then writes to his son's enemy and says, "*I think of him as my own son.*" Paul now allowed Philemon the opportunity to reconcile with his former slave, and to work together so that both men could fulfil their purpose, with a fresh relationship.

Fathers! Don't let days run into weeks and not contact your sons. Build a relationship with them, you have the technology that Paul and other fathers did not have.

The onus is on the fathers to bring restoration into the relationship between brothers. Paul didn't have the luxury or ability, because of incarceration, to get on a plane to bring both men to a place of reconciliation. Indeed he did the best he could, he wrote this beautiful letter and today we have the structure to be able to restore relationships.

Fathers' hearts turn to sons first, therefore the responsibility of any Apostolic Father is surely the ministry of reconciliation!

Loss of Communication Means Loss of a Relationship

Relationships are developed only one way, by communication. If a son or a father will not communicate, the relationship can never grow to the depth that is possible or desired by God It will finally disintegrate.

Communication takes time and patience. Father and son may not always agree but will allow for each other's character, nature, faults and failings and come to full acceptance of each other.

We must learn to love each other despite each other's negative imperfections and to embrace the positive.

It is important that each son communicates, not only with his spiritual father, but also with other siblings. Fathers must make time to develop and allow relationships within the family to blossom.

Just, as in Luke 11, the father's desire was that both sons develop an intimate relationship.

He asked the older son into the party explaining why he was developing the relationship with his younger son. It is important that fathers include their sons in each other's lives.

It is to be expected that if a father doesn't grant each son the same amount of time, then a sibling will experience feelings of rejection.

Results of Communication Loss

I write this from personal experience. In my own natural family, communication was not an element that we understood in our relationships. As siblings, when we matured and married we stopped communicating altogether as each of us isolated ourselves. Soon the lack of communication caused us to lose touch with each other and the days rolled into months and before long, years. Without even realizing it, when my older brother called me on Good Friday 2003, it was 20 years since we had last spoke! Now we are determined not to lose touch again and both of us know that the secret to this is *keep in touch regularly!*

Sadly, even in church families, I have seen the same thing happen. Perhaps because of hurt, illness or needing to isolate from the rest of the family, a sibling or father can remove himself from all contact. We must be realistic that this causes problems and will soon lead to the destruction of the relationship, hence the results are listed.

1) Breakdown of relationships. Best friends, even brothers, will soon become strangers. If we are not communicating, don't be deceived, we are neither relating nor connecting.

2) Seeds of mistrust are allowed to be planted and to grow. Neither brother will trust the other, and soon issues will be blown out of proportion.

3) Misinterpretation starts and soon assumptions are made based on behavior. Brothers start to look at things subjectively instead of objectively. Issues become personal and not decided as a team.

4) There is destruction of the transfer of knowledge, as was the case when the brothers attacked Joseph. For years, the family was not able to walk in its destiny because of this communication breach. It stifles, and will restrict growth of the family. All the information the father has now, cannot be imparted to his sons. All God given strategies are destroyed, as lack of communication has restricted impartation.

5) It will cause rejection and discouragement to breed in the family network.

6) It will sever the spirit of partnership which, if not restored, will be destroyed. Our resources that jointly affect the kingdom are no longer released.

7) It will create problems that, when compounded, will be extremely hard to mend, as it will be impossible to find the root.

8) Lack of communication can be a form of manipulation no different to a child who is not taught to communicate in an intelligent way. Instead, he cries and has a temper tantrum, and the result is that the parent gives in. This is not **communication**, it is **manipulation**! If left unchecked, it will cause the child to grow into a manipulating adult who will have "grown up" temper tantrums and be a controlling dictator, and not a leader. Let no conflict last longer than 24 hours. The Word says, *"Don't let the sun go down on your anger."* In other words, fix the problem, don't let it breed. When conflict is

left unchecked, the parties involved will always be in conflict and the conflict will eventually destroy what was once a good relationship.

Restoration of relationship is a major role of any father, allowing each one to communicate, and then bringing about reconciliation. Never let the problem become so big that in the end the issue becomes so immense that it becomes impossible to mend the relationship.

As I said above, this chapter is written from personal experience. How many can agree with me that they have lost dynamic, purpose filled relationships for two reasons? One, the problem was left to fester as a boil, and two, fathers didn't step in sooner.

It must never become about taking sides. Remember, in every situation there is a measure of truth on both sides and both may be right. The issue is coming into a place of agreement and restoration. When a father takes sides, he will now lose a son and a heritage. In a natural family we see this happen daily, and should a parent choose to side with one son over another, then the destiny of the whole family will be compromised.

This is not about spoils of war, that is the result of a warrior; it is about relationship above all else. We have seen too many apostolic fathers cut one son off without correct and proper procedures taking place through the process of mediation.

Again, this is not family, where relationships are restored, but a religious Mafia killing for the sake of the "family business!"

Remember don't ever fight for a cause, fight for relationship!

It is not the sibling rivalry that is the problem, but how we react to it, and how the father chooses to respond to it will be the factor that will decide the "fall out."

Sibling rivalry must become a process that will make their relationships grow and mature within each brother. We can see from Jonathan and David's relationship, that Jonathan could have been jealous of David. After all, Saul was Jonathan's father and Saul was king, so Jonathan should have been the next natural heir. Yet here was this shepherd boy chosen to lead the nation as king, and not the king's son. Jonathan could have chosen to be jealous and to take offense at David and, like his father, try to kill him, but he chose to allow the process to build their relationship, not break it.

It is up to the fathers to mediate through the restoration process. It is often futile to put some sons together in a room and say, "Sort it out!" How many of us parents would have had bloodshed if we had put our warring siblings together in our natural families and said, "Go for it!" Remember, some sons cannot live in the same house together. Is it wrong? No! If we have sons who have strong ministries, dominant personalities and stature, we may find a time of separation is needed until both are in the position to work together and not against each other.

We see here the John Mark factor. He was not strong enough to handle the apostolic pressure, but the man matured and the door was kept open for him to return. This was an example of family versus the apostolic.

Barnabas was related to John Mark and wanted to keep him on board for that reason, but Paul said he wanted good men. This caused strong disagreement because the result of blood family will be the outburst of strong principles. We need spiritual fathers who can cut through the natural bond of family and keep the spiritual family on track, not losing any but allowing the door of reconciliation to be kept open, as Paul did in this situation.

Relationship Brother to Brother.... The True Fruit of Fathering!

Every son must remember he is an individual. Each son has a different gift, talent, character, nature, personality and destiny. Don't try to compare one with another, let them get a revelation of their identity in Him. Each is different, and each positioned differently, each with his own destiny, and each will one day wear an individual crown.

On this day, Samuel arrived at Jesse's house to anoint one of his sons to be the next king. This crown was to become the lineage from which the King of Kings would come Eliab, a strapping, good looking young man, Jesse's eldest son. He was entitled to the inheritance and heritage because of his position as the eldest son. Samuel walks right past him, and Eliab watches in horror as his scrawny, smelly brother is called to the sacrifice, and what is more... Anointed!

Eliab, that day, allowed himself to give into wrong thought patterns which later governed his behavior. Jealousy, anger and rejection now cause a reaction toward his younger brother, instead of a response.

> *Eliab heard David talking to the men and was angry, "What are you doing here anyway?" he demanded "What about **those few sheep** you're supposed to be taking care of? I know about your pride and dishonesty. You just want to see the battle"* (1 Samuel 17:28). (Paraphrased)

The nation, including David's brothers, was at war with the Philistines, and Jesse asks David to take supplies to his brothers. They had been on the front lines for some time, facing the intimidating giant, Goliath, and were weary. David was a circumcised son; he knew the strength of the covenant made through circumcision. He arrives and sees his own brothers in mortal terror of this uncircumcised brute.

This Philistine had no covenant, and therefore no strength except that which was in his tongue. David asked what happens to the one who kills the Philistine, and his brother Eliab's heart rose in jealous rage.

What is sad is that Eliab discounted the fact that, although his brother was anointed king, and it was through David's lineage that the King of Kings would one day come, Eliab, though not necessarily named, would nevertheless be in the heritage and lineage of the coming Messiah.

Eliab had never been interested in his father's sheep; he had not been in the pasture protecting them.

Suddenly, Eliab in his rage, becomes territorial." Why did you come down here?" not even waiting to hear that the mission was one that his own father had ordained. Jealousy will always cause men and women to become territorial. Now he sees David come and attack his personal agenda, but doesn't see how they could work together as brothers.

His response to David was, *"With whom did you leave those few sheep in the wilderness?"* Those "few" sheep were not only his father's, but, because Eliab was the eldest they were also his heritage and inheritance.

By speaking in this derogative way about his father's sheep meant that Eliab was speaking against his own father and heritage!

We find in churches today, people rising up and becoming territorial–"this is my ministry" etc.

The story of David and Eliab, is a picture of true brotherly love. These were David's father's sheep and not only that, Eliab's inheritance as well, and yet David cared for them as his own. Here is a picture of wrong dynamics, yet if we look at Jonathan and David, we see the dynamics are wholesome. Jonathan, the king's son, did not at any time become territorial or self-protecting. His relationship was truly one of covenant, of what I have, is yours. Sadly, he did not exchange shoes in the cutting of the covenant. Shoes speak of destiny and if they had exchanged them, their connected destinies may have saved the young man.

The acid test in this new apostolic move is not just the relationship of father to son, but **the dynamic of brothers connecting to brothers!**

Two Kingdom Dynamics in Relationships

In our denominations, movements and networks, we are connected to each other because of the relationship we have in common with the one Father. We must be careful, because in the past we have built with wrong dynamics, bringing the patterns from dysfunctional relationships into the Body of Christ and then allowing the pattern of behavior to continue, building with the same dysfunctional dynamics.

Kingdom is family! The dynamic that put Jesus on the cross was family and this same dynamic brought many sons into the kingdom. While we are calling ourselves kingdom, and not using dynamics that will build **for** the kingdom, then we are building another organizational business.

We must transfer the new dynamics so that we develop and reproduce. A family is diverse, and it is in our diversity that we become one.

He who says he is in the light, and hates his brother, is in darkness until now (1 John 2:9).

If we do not walk in love as brother to brother, then we walk in darkness. If a church is operating under these dynamics then let's be honest, it is not a house, not a family and not even a church.

We will be no different to Eli officiating in the temple. Not only was the temple in darkness but soon he was also, and he became blind.

There is ... one Lord, one faith, one baptism; one God and Father of all, who is above all, and through all, and in you all. But to each one of us, grace was given according to the measure of Christ's gift (Ephesians 4:4-7).

Of whom (in Jesus Christ) *the whole family in heaven and earth is name.* (Ephesians 3:14-15).

This is where the strength of the family comes from, in oneness, and knowing that family is not an institution thought up by man, but it is a kingdom principle established by God. Family is not an organizational structure, but an organism that breathes and has the ability to produce life. This is why the enemy will do all he can to rip natural and spiritual families apart, because when he sees a family, he sees heaven, he sees the kingdom.

Intimate Covenant

Joseph was almost killed by his angry, territorial, self-protective brothers.

When Joseph finally revealed himself to his brothers after many years, we see a beautiful picture of covenant love and tenderness. When he showed his own brothers the covenant of circumcision, there was nothing for them to fear. (Genesis 45:1). We must go looking for our brethren and reveal covenant. We want a connection that removes the fear from one another. We want trust. If we have a covenant family where the fathers of the house are afraid to take the covenant knife and circumcise the sons, we will never remove the fear and bring back trust.

Joseph's brothers were so fearful of a backlash from him. But Joseph, in revealing his circumcision, let them know that they were the same. They were not only natural brothers, but they were in covenant with the same God. Within 24 hours, the influence of Joseph went from a tiny, filth-infested prison cell to the four corners of the earth. (Genesis 41:56). When there is intimate relationship and covenant, there is instant breakthrough.

Intimacy is in the seed in every son. Joseph could not restrain himself before all of those who stood before him, and he cried, *"Cause every man to go out from me. And there stood no man with him, while Joseph made himself known unto his brethren"* (Genesis 45:1).

The Hebrew word for **known** is **"yada"**. This is the Hebrew expression for the same word that Adam "knew" his wife.

It means to reveal oneself. God is restoring pure, covenant relationships in the Body of Christ.

> *To make all people see what is the fellowship of the mystery, which from the beginning of the ages has been hidden in God...* (Ephesians 3:9).

The revelation of this intimate relationship, is the fellowship that Paul talks about here. Adam and Eve were so connected, and God and Adam were also connected in the same manner. In Philippians 2:1 when Paul says, *"If there is any fellowship of the spirit,"* he is not speaking about just fellowship with God in the Spirit, but also with those who are family, brother to brother, and it is because we are connected that we must fellowship. In verse 2, he goes onto say "being like-minded," the same word he used when speaking about his relationship with Timothy, and the same as Adam's relationship with God and then his relationship with Eve.

Verse 15 tells us that church is a family, connected in fellowship, like-minded and knowing each other intimately. Perhaps, like me, you are asking, where on the planet does such a church really exist? Most churches are religious organizations with the same murderous spirit that was in the first brother to brother dispute.

It is time to change the pattern and building according to eternal design. Remember you are fearfully and wonderfully made, you are unique, your sibling, though not like you, compliments you. Family is more than a name; it is a group of individuals passionately seeking to make another's dream a reality. At age thirty, Jesus could have disconnected from His father and changed the world Himself. Such was the dynamic within Him, yet He did nothing unless he had first heard from His Father.

Relate and communicate with each other. If Cain had communicated with Abel, and if Joseph's brothers had communicated with Joseph, circumstances may have changed. If Jesus' brothers had communicated with Him instead of just seeing Him as Joseph's son, how differently they would have seen things. Why didn't they ever sit with Him and asked Him to divulge His innermost secrets to them? Would history be different today?

There was John, the cousin of Jesus, who had the chance to learn the secrets of heaven as they grew together, but instead, as John was about to be martyred, he asked his disciples to check if Jesus really was the Son of God.

We are hearing in churches such statements as these "God is purging His church", or "God is sifting and ridding His church of the dross." Please pastors, **WAKE UP**, realize what you are saying. Does a father purge his own family, ridding it of unwanted waste?! This is what the Mafia does when you are no longer needful to the family.

Does a father slam the door behind a son and say, "I'm glad he has gone"? We are not an organization where we "trim the top off management overload."

We are the family NAMED after the family in heaven! We must seek for more revelation of this and receive stronger dynamics to break old patterns and establish new ones.

3 Keys to a Family

1) Communicate with each other.

Find out what makes each person tick. Find out each other's dreams and visions, their strengths and their limitations.

2) Build the relationship with the commodity called time.

Don't expect to have a good relationship if neither party ever takes time out to build. Never use the excuse "I don't have time," such a lame excuse will be the cause of strife. If you don't have time for your family then you don't deserve the revelation of the family God has given you. Tough words? Yes, because we don't want to see another son or father wounded by family strife again. We long to see whole families in these last days, so that we, the Body of Christ can show the world what a family really is. If you don't live close to your spiritual family, a quick e-mail every week or phone call is an easy means of contact. Don't expect to build a strong relationship if you don't communicate!

3) Treat each individual with the honor they deserve, and each individual's dream due the honor and respect owed, in the sanctity from whence it came. Honor is a sadly lacking commodity in families today; we should fight to bring it back.

In the movie "Braveheart" the leading character William Wallace, stands and declares, "It is better to die with honor than to live without it!"

David honored his friend and covenant brother so highly that this honor extended from the grave into another generation. When David heard that his covenant brother's son was still alive, he gave the same honor to this young man as he had to his father. He restored to him all that was owed to him. Honor is a powerful spiritual principle that extends to generations to come. You cannot make a covenant, nor keep it, if honor is not the basic ingredient.

The Word says, *"If we honor our fathers and mothers, then we live long on the earth."* This was the first commandment that had a covenant promise. This should be extended to our spiritual fathers as well. It seems that those in ministry have a "used by date" on their usefulness. Could this be the reason that so many ministries fail, due to the obvious lack of honor?

We see today, our teenagers sitting on a bus when an elderly man or woman is left to stand; you walk through a door and are pushed out of the way as a youngster walks in front of you. What have we produced in our society? No more than a rebellious generation with no honor for the past generations.

Could this lack of honor have had its roots in the church? Perhaps as we rushed to remove the last generation by throwing out the fathers of the ministry once they reached their "used by date," we actually broke a covenant promise. We thought of the younger men in ministry, about how much more they would relate to the next generation, and all we did was to deplete ourselves of power, as the two go hand in hand.

What an honor the spiritual fathers of today have. Sons, honor the fathers in the Body of Christ, and treat them with the dignity and respect they deserve. Daniel was known, not for his incredible speeches but because he was a man of honor and integrity. This must become our character trait and lifestyle. These two qualities are what ultimately allowed him to seize his destiny. Even if the fathers in the Body are older and have now stepped out of pulpit ministry, let us honor these men, for surely it is through them that the way was paved for us to pursue the purpose of God.

Fathers, bless your sons; this gives them a dimension in Christ, a stature and confidence that we have not tapped into yet and yet most of all, communicate with them for without this dynamic, all else is futile.

Chapter Thirteen

Building the Apostolic into Our Churches to Produce a Kingdom Philosophy.

The path of a pioneer is not an easy one. We can't even consider becoming a governing territorial church without first being able to govern our own lives. Today, leaders are rising up and breaking-through into new dimensions of the spirit so the next generation can go in, possess the land and walk in the miraculous, naturally.

Pioneers are the ones who are the spotless, wrinkle free bride, who have matured and entered into a place of manhood. God wants a pure message coming from a wholesome messenger. It will not come through creams and potions but the quickening spirit that rests on pioneers, to bring us into breakthrough after breakthrough. A pioneer's road is one of loneliness and isolation, but also a place of immense victory.

God is sending the revelation of sons to break the paradigm of leadership structure we have in our churches today. The early church was birthed on discipleship, but when we read further into the epistles, the word "disciple" is not used readily and we see the emergence of a new word, "sons". As the church matured, **it was birthed by fathers and led by sons.**

To breakthrough the leadership structure that is in place at the moment, fathers and sons have to be pioneers and have certain characteristics that separate them from those who are settlers, those who are benefiting from what pioneers of past generations have accomplished. Settlers and squatters have been building denominations for decades. They found a well, pitched their tent and stayed there!

Pioneers braved the harsh elements to discover new regions that had not yet been discovered. Squatters on the other hand, would take the land already developed by the settlers and give nothing back to the land, paying no rent or tax.

Apostolic men and women are like the pioneers. They will take on the new frontiers and build on the unknown territory leaving behind a legacy for the generations to follow.

Settlers on the other hand, are happy for others to go before them, to continue to build, develop and maintain the production where another started. We need both settlers and pioneers so as to build a heritage for the next generation to live in and continue to build on. Squatters on the other hand, will put nothing into the place they inhabit and soon they will leave the place of residence and move on.

Psalm 42:7 says, *"Deep calls unto deep."* Could it be that the revelation of past generations is calling to the pioneers of this generation? The psalmist goes onto say, *"All your waves and billows have gone over me."* The pioneer must wade through the turmoil that will come as the church plots a course of change so that the future sons can move in it.

Pioneers are not happy to stay as part of the status quo that past generations have created, but are willing to set off into the waves and billows to blaze a new path for future sons to follow. No matter how hard the environment, let us pioneering fathers and sons, break through every new path so it is developed for the church to move forward.

Pioneers today are creating new dimensions for the church to walk in and we must remember that we are making the way for the revelation of the family to be absorbed. Not only so the church can move in this dimension, but so that the structure and fabric of society can change. God said in Malachi that before Jesus returned, *"The hearts of the fathers be turned to the sons and the hearts of the sons, be turned toward the fathers."* Let us see this scripture in greater detail.

Reformation is not just so we can turn our people from being attendees to sons, but so the benchmark that society is ruled by can be changed and reformed.

The church must set the standard that society is to be governed by, not society setting the standard for the church. We have seen a decline in our society with the family pattern being eroded and it must be by the church setting the standard, that we transform our culture. No longer will it be humanistic, but kingdom!

Fathers and sons have an innate ability to infuse hope, encouragement and inspiration into people, causing them to move ahead and not be wedged into yesterday.

The quickening spirit that is upon fathers and sons brings about breakthrough that allows people to fulfill the purpose of God that is within their heart and see the destiny of this generation fulfilled.

Within the dynamic of each man's vision, is the ability to keep the people restrained and controlled, as we see in Psalm 29:18, *"Where there is no, vision, the people are unrestrained."* Fathers and sons have the ability to keep a prophetic vision fresh in people's hearts and in so doing, keep the people restrained and on the path of righteousness. The same internal dynamic within a vision that restrains people, also has the capability to bring it to pass.

The apostolic anointing that is on a pioneering father is there to break through during the hard times of opposition and resistance. It is during these hard times that the load of the vision can seem like a burden, and the father at this time must be careful not to allow discouragement, hurts and bitterness to deplete his strength. Opposition to the vision will always come, but the end result is how we choose to deal with it. We must be careful not to duplicate a father's negative response during times of stress. A pioneering father must teach his son how to respond during the difficult times when he is establishing new places in God.

If he begins to internalize his own weaknesses, he will disintegrate under the burden he is called to bear, and often this leads to denial of the problem. It is at this point that the father will compromise his call and vision and thus causing the son to feel insecure and discouraged.

Fathers make the mistakes so that the sons of tomorrow don't have to repeat history and destroy their own destiny. We see even in the present generation, how one father did not accomplish the demise of an ungodly government, ruled by a "father," controlling not only a civilization, but a society. We see how his son, when he came into power, had to deal with the "spiritual father and his sons" of this ungodly reign.

We must do more than just bless our sons and begin to impart a concept of building. It is imperative that we recognize that, by keeping a theory whereby people are continually blessed, is to keep the church in a state of dependence. The church has tried to build by teaching a dogma of a blessing mentality and we have created nothing more than weak Christians. It is sad that instead of the prosperity message allowing us to reform society, we have fashioned a people striving to better each other through material possessions.

When our people take hold of the concept of building, they then see themselves as living stones building the temple of God.

We must realize that it is not the stones that keep the walls from falling apart, but the mortar between them, and the mortar is connection and relationship without which we can build nothing. It is only when we build relationships with each other that we then need not worry about another trying to take his authority and causing strife within the house.

We must take our people past the concept of just receiving a blessing. The Word says the rain falls on the just and the unjust. Even the unrighteous walk in the blessings–even nature itself lives off the blessings of God. We must take them into a new dimension where they live not from blessing to blessing, but in their inheritance. When the Israelites entered the wilderness, they learnt to have their daily needs met. God wanted them to walk in their rightful inheritance and fulfil His purposes as a people and a nation. God wanted the fathers to walk them into their promised land and then rule it.

Our forefathers have built many monuments to their past triumphs and victories. Though beautiful, they are now irrelevant to the future generations and they have become a place to remember death, and not the living truth.

Tradition keeps us focused on man made ideals, and on men. We must remember that we are all different, we think, look and talk differently. Let us not focus on the differences but on the connection we have in Christ.

We may not always agree, but let us remember this. No matter what title we have been given, whether pastor, apostle or father, it does not give us the right to eradicate and cut another off.

How desperately you fight for relationship, will be the proof of the depth that covenant means to you. If we fight for **our** cause and agenda, then truly our understanding of the patterned Son's last words at His covenant meal have not become ours.

A vision must be one, complete with a God given mandate, or else it becomes a powerless empty vessel.

A mandate with the absence of fathering, becomes a structure with a controlling religious governmental order being its strength and not the **covenant relationship** between family.

A Religious Mafia

The title of this book asked if we were the family of God or a religious Mafia. The concept of the family of God has been sufficiently covered in the above chapters, but perhaps we should cover the regulations concerning the Mafia to have a true understanding and make an intelligent judgement.

Mafia families became extremely territorial and each family bore the name of the place they occupied. Each family was an entity within itself and there was great competition between families.

The Mafia controlled every aspect of a person's life, their money, their family, their relationships and friendships. Even where and how they lived, was passed by the head of the family before approval was given. If one of the family wished to marry, permission and approval had to be sought by the family head and then the relationship governed by rules and regulations. Each friendship and relationship went under intense scrutiny by the family head and ultimately was allowed or disconnected.

The Mafia penetrated every strata of society, social, political and cultural etc. The families would introduce a sub-culture where all women where excluded. They internalized their relationships, all must be approved of and soon they began using their own language and belief system. When the Mafia mobster Scafidi, a fourth generation criminal took the stand, he sobbed as he broke the Mafia's code of silence and spoke about the family's beliefs. He was devastated that he had to destroy a heritage that had been built over generations.

As a church family we too can work together, this is not the issue though. Where do we draw the line in suspecting or accusing each other of complicity in or alluding to a Mafia style organization?

The answer is simple: *"Where the Spirit of the Lord is, there is liberty."* As we build together, the Spirit of the Lord must be the centrality of our construction and therefore we will have liberty in our relationships. To build a family home we must have fathers who are willing to submit to their heavenly Father and allow the Spirit of the Lord to rule and reign in the relationships. Those who will take their sons further than they themselves can run and allow them to walk into a heritage and inheritance that they themselves have worked to erect.

In saying that ……

Let us also cry with the Apostle Paul…

"Where are the fathers?"

Surely Lord, let Thy will be done and let them come Lord Jesus, let them come!! Amen and Amen.

A CALL TO THE SECRET PLACE
By Michal Ann Goll

Deep inside each one of us is a longing to escape the frantic pace of life in the 21st Century.

A Call to the Secret Place is your personal invitation to take that step towards the place lovingly prepared for you. Cheering you on will be the voices of other women as shared by Michal Ann Goll, women on the frontlines like Madam Guyon, Susanna Wesley, Fanny Crosby, Basilea Schlink, Gwen Shaw, Beth Alves and others. Their collective voices call out inviting you to join them in the privacy of a loving moment with your Lord.
ISBN: 0-7684-2179-9

THE ETERNAL CHURCH
By Bill Hamon

Dr. Bill Hamon takes you on a journey throughout the history of the church. Beginning at the origination of the church in the first century, he proceeds to the deterioration of the church during the Middle Ages, the restoration of the church from the time of the reformation to present. He also explores the eternal destination of the church in the years to come including the eternal ages.

This unique perspective shows graphically the 'whys' as well as the 'whats' of church history. Bill Hamon is a valid modern prophet who writes the story of the Church of Jesus Christ from the perspective of one who sees not only the past, but has glimpses into the future.
ISBN:0-7684-2176-4

Order Now To Destiny Image Europe:
Telephone: +39 085 4220170 – Fax +39 085 4220168
E-mail: ordini@eurodestinyimage.com
Internet: www.eurodestinyimage.com

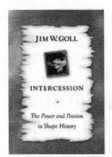

INTERCESSION
By Jim W. Goll

The words of the intercessor are a power force for healing the wounds of the past and shaping the course of history. This book will help the intercessor release those words into the heavens and bring down God's will on earth.

Goll shifts the focus of intercession away from the typical 'shot gun' approach of praying for the whole world in a single prayer. At the same time he impressively portrays how you can focus your prayer on what God desires as opposed to what you need.

ISBN: 0-7684-2184-5

ISRAEL THE CHURCH AND THE LAST DAYS
By Keith Intrater and Dan Juster

The Last Days is a topic of great controversy in the church today. Does Israel have a place in the end times? Is the Kingdom now or future or both? Does the church escape, take over or go down in defeat? Is there a millennial age. These and many other questions are examined in the light of the Scriptures and present day events.

ISBN. ISBN. 0-7684-2187-X

Order Now To Destiny Image Europe:
Telephone: +39 085 4220170 – Fax +39 085 4220168
E-mail: ordini@eurodestinyimage.com
Internet: www.eurodestinyimage.com

Additional copies of this book and other book titles from DESTINY IMAGE EUROPE are available at your local bookstore.

For a complete list of our titles, visit us at:

www.eurodestinyimage.com

Send a request for a catalog to:

C.so V.Emanuele, 10

65121 PESCARA – ITALY